THE TECHNIQUE OF MOTOR RACING

THE
TECHNIQUE
OF
MOTOR RACING

PIERO TARUFFI

TRANSLATED FROM THE ITALIAN BY

D. B. TUBBS
'King Pin' of *The Motor*

ROBERT BENTLEY, INC.
CAMBRIDGE, MASSACHUSETTS

First published in England 1959
Second impression 1960
Third impression 1964
Fourth impression 1966
Fifth impression 1969
Sixth impression 1971
Seventh impression 1974
Eighth impression 1978
Ninth impression 1989

TYPOGRAPHY BY ANTHONY BROWN

Library of Congress Catalogue Card Number 60-1662
ISBN 8376-0228-9
Manufactured in the United States of America

ACKNOWLEDGEMENTS

THE PUBLISHERS acknowledge with thanks the valuable help and advice given by Harry Mundy and Peter Garnier of *The Autocar*, D. B. Tubbs of *The Motor*, George Phillips of *Autosport*, for the jacket photograph, and the following photographers whose pictures appear in this book: Bernard Cahier, Coccia, John Deacon, Fumigalli, Rudolfo Mailander, Argo Milano, Corrado Millanta, Foto News, Offolenghi, Perrucci, Publifoto, Sgattoni and Sandro Vespasiani.

CONTENTS

FOREWORD

by JUAN MANUEL FANGIO

MANY BOOKS have been written about motor racing, each helping in some way to increase the appreciation of what I consider to be the greatest sport in the world. But all these books have been directed at the general public; this is the first I have seen that has been written for the drivers themselves—a text-book on motor racing. I am glad that it should have been by Piero Taruffi—at one time or another my team mate, co-driver, or rival, but always friend. I do not think anyone is better qualified to write such a book, for he has not only the trained mathematician's approach but the experience of years from which to draw his conclusions. The grey hairs, which have made him give up racing, are an advantage when it comes to passing on one's experience to the coming generation!

I have had the advantage of seeing him 'at work' perhaps more than any other single person. In 1952 we were teamed together with Castellotti, Bonetto, and Bracco in the great Carrera Panamericana road race, driving 3.3-litre Lancia sports cars. Poor Bonetto lost his life in that event, but three of the Lancias, driven by myself, Piero, and Castellotti, went on to take first three places. In 1955 we were again teamed together, driving for Mercédès-Benz, when he took second place to me in the Italian Grand Prix. As rivals we met on many occasions, but one I remember best was the Swiss Grand Prix of 1951, when he was driving a big, heavy, 4½-litre Ferrari and I the splendid little Tipo 159 Alfa Romeo. I was fortunate enough to win, but behind me there developed a wonderful struggle between Piero's Ferrari and Farina's 159 Alfa—which brought the crowds to their feet, and stole my limelight. On the last, dramatic lap the Alfa, trying to pass the Ferrari, slid off the road, finally finishing third, only 25 seconds behind Piero.

As co-drivers, we paired up in the 1954 Tourist Trophy, after my own car had broken down. The sports car regulations were different in those days; I took over from Piero's co-driver Piodi, and together we went on to finish fourth on handicap with the 3.3-litre Lancia.

In years of experience I think he beats us all—from his first win, in 1923 to his final victory for Ferrari in the 1957 Mille Miglia; it was always his ambition to win this event, one of the great, open road races that are no more. The value of these years of experience when passed on to the younger generation is tremendous—but it is rare that the hand that holds the steering wheel can do equal justice to the pen. Taruffi is fortunate in having both these gifts; his assessment of the qualities necessary for success is the best I have seen, and he is right in putting enthusiasm first. Without it, the other qualities, however great, are valueless.

A young driver's progress will be greatly assisted by taking his advice, and absorbing all he has to say, not only about the technical aspects but the many other sides of motor racing with which he deals. The rest lies in a man's own personal make-up—those peculiar, intangible assets of mind and body which no text-book can describe, no formula resolve, but which provide the final inspiration . . . the stock-in-trade of the great driver.

I

NECESSARY QUALITIES

I HAD meant to say that motor racing is a sport that cannot be taught; but I think this view is mistaken, for one has only to look around at the world of sport to see the number of coaching and training establishments that exist, each giving instruction in its chosen field, to see that a course of lessons is the best and quickest method of getting results.

In my time I have gone in for many sports, apart from motor racing, and in these I have always tried to start off with an instructor. It has always paid. When it came to motoring, however, there was no school, and I had to work everything out for myself: I spent a lot of time discovering exactly what to do, and often paid dearly for mistakes that I might never have made had there been anybody to give me advice, especially on technical matters. Now, at the end of my career as a driver, therefore, I have decided to pass on what I know. I hope that it will be useful, particularly to the younger enthusiast and to those who want to know how to become a racing driver.

Motor racing entails many risks, both personal and financial; therefore I do most strongly advise anyone who decides to take it up seriously to make sure that he has the right qualities.

Experience shows that the would-be driver, if he is to obtain reasonable results, must have more than a fair share of the following:

1 Great enthusiasm;
2 A sizeable helping of courage, and mastery over his nerves;
3 The right mental and physical make-up;
4 Physical fitness and lots of stamina;
5 A good bank balance.

Besides the above qualifications, all of which except the last can be described as natural gifts, it is well to have an understanding of things mechanical, and, more important still, of the technique of handling a racing car. I should also perhaps add another factor that often comes into it, especially in the case of young drivers: a sympathetic family background. In my own case I could not have been more fortunate: my father encouraged me to take up every kind of sport, and, in particular, motor-cycling. Any success that I have earned I owe to him, and I can never be grateful enough. I can only wish that every young rider may be equally fortunate.

Let us look at our list of qualities. First: enthusiasm. Ask any first-class sportsman, and I do not mean merely in motor racing, and he will tell you that unless you have great enthusiasm you will never do really well. Enthusiasm, or as we Italians say, 'passion', means believing utterly in what you are doing; it means self sacrifice, an ability to adapt oneself to circumstances, and the will to keep cheerful even in the blackest moments. The real enthusiast must be willing to play a waiting game, and able to 'write off' in his own mind, any successes that come his way, and concentrate on how to do even better in future.

But this is only the beginning. You need also courage and good nerves; courage to jump back into the car after a 'shunt' and not want to bail out at the first untoward noise; and calm nerves to cope efficiently with all the sudden and exciting situations that crop up during a race, especially at very high speeds.

We now come to the psychophysical requirements. Every candidate should undergo a searching medical examination, with special attention to the eyes, being tested for colour-blindness, 'tunnel vision', night sight, and so on. The doctor examining a driver's cardio-vascular system will not only look out for the classic symptoms of weak heart, but he will make sure that that organ is capable of bearing the emotional strains inseparable from motor racing. The apparatus that looks after one's sense of balance must also be checked, particularly the labyrinth of the inner ear and the semi-circular canals, and also that deep muscular co-ordination which helps to produce a 'sense of position'. A driver stimulates these in many circumstances—principally when braking or accelerating hard, or when subject to centrifugal forces. They are of the utmost importance, because it is they which let him know when the car is about to 'break away'. A car at speed is constantly being affected by outside forces tending to throw it off course, and the driver's job is to bring it back into the correct line by continual movements of the steering-wheel. He has therefore to be extraordinarily sensitive to every movement his car makes, for it is these movements, transmitted to his body, which are picked up and interpreted by the 'deep muscular sensibility' and the balance mechanism of the ears. The driver then has to translate these external stimuli into the action needed to correct the course of the car. The length of time he takes to do this is called his 'reaction time'. It is worth having your reaction time measured on one of the machines designed for this purpose, and to ascertain also the effects of fatigue upon your quickness to react.

No need to labour the medical aspect; but I do want to underline its importance. Average results in these tests are perfectly adequate for ordinary motoring, but must be considered utterly insufficient for those who drive really fast cars, not only for their own sake but for that of other people.

If one's gifts in this direction are only moderate it need not exclude one entirely from motor racing. Championship honours will be 'out', but even quite gentle racing can be fun.

Anyone taking up racing must have certain physical attributes and plenty of stamina. I think, though, that any youngster who is healthy and physically fit can, with suitable coaching, acquire all that it takes; I deal with the means more fully in a later chapter.

As regards intelligence, this is so much taken for granted in every human activity that it would be strange indeed if it were not also required in racing which demands not only courage but liveliness, quick thinking, acute psychological analysis, mechanical sense, good memory and a tidy mind. A driver's ability to weigh up the possibilities, solve the various pre-race problems, and settle tactics during the race itself, can make all the difference in a race.

Unfortunately these qualities are not much good unless they are accompanied by a pretty large private bank balance; you will not find other people anxious to entrust you with a car costing thousands of pounds. The lucky exceptions are those who have a job as mechanic or tester in a factory connected with racing. This gives them the opportunity to handle fast cars, and from them—at small cost to himself—a future champion may emerge.

Another way of making good with a minimum of expense is to start by racing motor-cycles. I think it is true to say that this sport costs only a fifth as much as car racing, although requiring and developing the same gifts. By starting on bikes you can save yourself a good deal of expense during the training period. Varzi and Nuvolari, to name only the most famous, were first of all great motor-cycling champions. I too served a long apprenticeship on two wheels and as a result of my motor-cycle racing I was invited to try my hand at cars.

Apart from these two solutions, I do not for the moment see any other, unless the national bodies governing motor sport, or private enterprise, give their support to the development of ever more economical racing cars, and put these at the disposal of the young drivers deemed most fit to handle them. The development of Formula 2 and Formula Junior might well provide the answer.

2

PHYSICAL TRAINING AND CLOTHING

P ART OF my success as a racing driver I owe to the careful physical training that I have always imposed upon myself. In my view this training should be fairly general in character. You need to enjoy good health, and for this you should lead a sane, restful sort of life, free from worries that can play on your nerves. Start a race already tired and not on top of your form mentally and physically, and you carry a handicap that can cost you—probably without your realizing it—precious time that cannot be made up.

Everyone knows what we mean by a sane sort of life: keeping proper control over sleeping, eating, and . . . Bacchus, baccy and Venus!

Proper physical training will greatly improve your performance. In motor racing as in other sports certain muscles and organs are placed under an extra strain; so it is logical to exercise these specially and get them under control. The muscles which do most work are those in the shoulders and the arms: the deltoids and the biceps and the muscles of the forearm. The leg muscles have little to do, except when the brakes require heavy pressure, or during long races where great use has to be made of the brakes. The body muscles take considerable punishment when travelling over bumpy roads. All exercises that develop the above muscles are to be recommended. To improve your grip and the action of the wrists use a spring exerciser. I remember that Achille Varzi used to spend several minutes every day screwing up newspaper in his hands to improve his grip and harden the palms.

'Press-Ups' and exercises in the gym (fig. 1) strengthen the deltoids and biceps. Stretching exercises with a spring exerciser are excellent too. You can develop your 'brake muscles' by doing some 'knees bend' (fig. 2). Bending and twisting the torso exercises the trunk muscles (fig. 3); twisting the head helps to build up the neck muscles (fig. 4). These are the exercises to do if you confine yourself to indoor gymnastics.

Rowing, which I myself have gone in for, is one of the best forms of exercise: it develops the legs, the arms and the body, and hardens the hands as well. If you exercise upon an indoor rowing machine in a very hot room

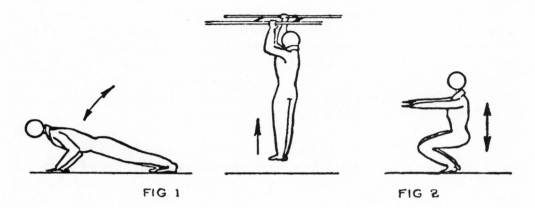

FIG 1   FIG 2

it will harden you against the strains of racing in hot climates and in motor cars with bad cockpit ventilation. To training of this sort with the temperature over 95°F. I owe my endurance in races held under similar conditions.

To develop rapid reflexes take part in any of the sports demanding a quick eye and rapid decisions: tennis (especially doubles), trap-shooting, etc.

FIG 3   FIG 4

Another excellent all round sport, and one that has an affinity with motor racing, is skiing: downhill to get used to speed; slalom, for the technique of cornering; climbing for the legs, the arms, and for hardening the palms. And of course, bob-sleighing which can be called 'motoring on ice'. In bobbing, if you have not superlatively sensitive powers of balance, you haven't a chance. You quickly become expert at banked

15

corners and learn to take them without 'raking' and so with the minimum loss of energy and speed. There is no engine on a sleigh to replace the speed you have lost, so bobbing is a good lesson in cornering technique for racing drivers.

If you can compete so much the better. You will get used to the thrills of racing and be able to find your form under the most varying conditions. Also you will manage to overcome difficulties which, in normal conditions, would probably be too much for you. In short, you will learn to be a fighter. Competition will teach you to pare away split seconds, and to seize any opportunity of doing so. You will also learn to size up your opponents, and to behave towards them in a thoroughly sporting way.

CLOTHING   Clothing and equipment should be kept in perfect condition; this can mean the difference between winning and losing a race. In open cars goggles are most important. Take great care in choosing the right type; the quality of the glass or plastic lens should be such that there is no refraction or distortion of the image, because even if imperceptible this can tire the eyes, especially in a long race. Rest the eyes: this means dark goggles for bright sunshine. In long road races I used a leather eyeshade to cut off the direct rays of the sun, especially at dawn and sunset. This probably prevented my going off the road, and my eyes were much less tired at the finish.

It is important for the goggles to be well ventilated, otherwise they steam up with perspiration. It is best to put them on as late as possible before the start of a race; 15–20 seconds before the 'off' gives you time to adjust them properly and get into gear. If, as I know from experience, you put them on before this, they will be liable to mist up as the flag falls. To avoid this you should wipe over the inside of the lenses with an anti-misting preparation. The latter is essential when it's raining as glasses then steam up much more easily; also, in the wet it is wise to cover the ventilation holes on top of the goggles to stop rain driving in. In very heavy rain and in poor lights, is it safer to use a visor of the all-round type. Do not wait until the race to try out these modifications; do it beforehand, during practice. In an open car always keep a piece of chamois leather or soft paper handy for cleaning your goggles: it often happens that a fly elects to get squashed at the precise point that you wish to look through. The polisher should preferably have been soaked in a liquid detergent to make it act quickly, and it should always be stowed within easy reach, so that you do not have to drive one-handed for too long. It should be fixed somewhere where it cannot blow away, and where it will not pick up grease and smear the goggles. Wipe little and often, so that a film of dirt never has time to form, and do one side first and then the other. Do take trouble to follow this advice and get

Above: The author's début as a racing driver, using the 'family barouche'—a Fiat 501 S, in the Rome–Viterbo race of 1923. He is seen with his father, who acted as his adviser and passenger in this first victorious sortie.

ow: Monza, 1931. Taruffi on the 500 Norton on which he averaged 103 m.p.h. for 100 kilometres and set a new lap ord of more than 106 m.p.h. It was after this performance that Enzo Ferrari invited him to try one of his Alfa-Romeos.

II.

Above : Taruffi taking part in the slalom event at Bardonecchia for the Italian Universities Ski Championships 1933, in which he was placed second.

Below : 'Motor racing' on ice. Taruffi on the bob-sleigh run at Cortina d'Ampezzo.

properly fixed up; it really is worth while, because dirty goggles can lose you seconds during a race without your realizing it. It is worth while carrying a spare pair of goggles, in some place where they will keep clean but can be easily got at. Some drivers wear them round the neck, but this is not a good idea as they may pick up dirt. Experienced drivers carry a whole selection around with them in the little bag that goes with them to every race meeting, holding their crash helmet and gloves, competition licence, a card showing their blood group, and a whole host of other useful tackle—not forgetting a little First Aid outfit.

Another extremely important accessory, upon which one's life can depend, is the crash helmet. Choose a type which provides the maximum protection without being unduly heavy. These sound conflicting requirements but there are certain experienced makers who manage to combine the two. The outer shell should be proof against shocks and able to deaden them, while the internal air-space should be so arranged as to cushion the shock in the event of a crash, transforming a sharp localized blow into gentler pressure dispersed over the whole head. In the best helmets the outside is made from numerous thicknesses of cloth glued over a light crown made of cork. There should be a future for plastics. The air-chamber, either constructed from strong strips of leather or made as a linen cap, should be adjustable so that the helmet can be set to the right height. This cap part must be very strong, and very firmly attached, especially the part that goes under the chin. What a lot of accidents there have been through the driver losing his helmet at the moment of impact! There should be hooks at the back or sides for attaching the goggles, and adequate circulation of air will ward off sunstroke during very hot weather. A helmet for use in closed cars can be much lighter, especially when the driver wears safety harness, so as to avoid causing headaches. Whatever happens, resist the temptation to take the thing off!

In racing cars, where there is always a lot of exhaust noise, it is a good thing to wear ear-plugs made of rubber or wax—or simply cotton-wool—otherwise you will probably be deaf for hours after the race. It is essential to wear gloves; but thick palms will affect the sensitivity of your handling of the wheel, especially on cars with very light steering. The amount of work with the gear-lever in racing is considerable and, unless you have worked away at your hands until they are very hard and horny, gloves will prevent the formation of blisters. In driving cars with a very heavy gear-change, the hand that works the lever should be well protected, even if this means wearing bits of sticking-plaster here and there; and the lever, too, may be fitted with a rubber knob. Sometimes, at the end of a long-distance race, I have heard drivers complain that their hands were so sore for the last few miles that they could not steer the car.

With regard to clothing, I recommend overalls fitting tightly at wrists and ankles, and held in at the waist with an elastic belt, to prevent 'ballooning' at speed. I also like elastic round the pockets, to make them easy to get at. As for fastenings in general, I have no preference as between buttons and 'zippers'. I myself generally wear linen trousers with pockets at knee height, where I can reach them easily when sitting at the wheel, and a woollen jersey with long sleeves. It is wise to make sure that all garments, including socks, are made of material not easily affected by fire. Avoid wearing nylon next to the skin as, although not very inflammable, it melts when exposed to heat and causes most horrible burns; it can however be worn over other garments. Pure wool, on the other hand, is splendidly resistant to fire. You can buy special stuff for fire-proofing clothing, and do it yourself at home.

The best kind of shoes for driving have soles made of leather, because rubber gets slippery when oily or wet, and an interlining of asbestos between the soles to protect you from the heat coming up through the pedals. This extra thickness is also valuable in insulating the feet from vibration, which can be troublesome in long-distance races. My own choice of footwear is a kind of shoe, or rather a kind of low boot, based on those used by boxers. Suitably altered these answer very well.

In wet weather a waterproof jacket is sufficient to protect the parts that are most exposed; I do not recommend completely water-proofed overalls because they stop the air circulating, making you sweat and increasing fatigue.

To protect the kidneys, which otherwise are subjected to a lot of road-shocks, I recommend an elastic body-belt, fitting tightly round the waist.

In long and tiring races you should do something about provisions. Have some lumps of sugar (or other more effective source of energy) within reach of your hand. In hot climates carry a thermos of whatever drink you fancy: cold tea, for example. You drink through a long flexible pipe leading to the flask, which must be solidly attached and insulated from shock.

3

THE DRIVING POSITION

IF YOU are not comfortably seated you cannot give of your best; and you are a potential menace to yourself and other people. Everyone, and especially racing drivers, should pay great attention to seating.

THE SEAT The brakes, centrifugal force while cornering, and bumpiness of the road, tend to throw you in three different directions, with forces which often reach a value equivalent to your own weight. It is the seat that has to absorb all these forces.

To resist the force of inertia during braking that tends to throw you forwards, the seat cushion should slope upwards towards the front; to oppose the centrifugal cornering forces, it should come up to give lateral support round the thighs while leaving ample freedom of movement for the arms.

To cope with these forces drivers are often apt to hang on to the wheel. Never, never do this, because it causes inadvertent movements of the steering, and puts the car off its proper line.

A belt, or better still a pair of straps passing over the shoulders and securely anchored to the seat, will limit the amount of vertical displacement due to bumps, and I recommend such a shoulder-harness in closed cars too, as it prevents your head from striking the roof in the event of a crash. An aviation type harness is the best, and it should be provided with a quick-release catch. American drivers wear them even in open cars. I do not want to express an opinion, although I did use them at Monza in 1934, driving a 3-litre *monoposto* Maserati, and found them an advantage, especially on the rather bumpy patches on the banking.

In the absence of a harness, the best way to hold oneself firmly against the leaping of a fast car on bad surfaces is to point the left foot and press it hard down on the floor, so that the body is braced firmly between the footboard and the squab of the seat. To resist lateral forces it is a good plan to have a padded rest for the right leg attached to the inside of the body. In this way you are held immovably, so far as that's possible, and can move your arms freely without outside forces affecting the steering.

AT THE WHEEL   How far to sit from the steering-wheel is a matter of personal preference, and less debatable now than it was at one time. In the past, drivers sat much closer to the wheel, with the arms well bent, so as to exert the maximum muscular force. Today, when steerings are much lighter, the most usual attitude is the one popularized by Nuvolari, that is to say with arms almost straight. It is the most restful, and excellent for holding the body pressed back into the squab of the seat. Sitting like this, one can counteract the inertia of the body, as it is thrown forward or sideways while braking or cornering, without involuntarily turning the wheel. The steering-wheel rim should be slightly rough and wavy, and the driver's hands should rest upon it at the same height on the left side as on the right. Or to put this more clearly: if the wheel is regarded as the face of a clock, the driver's hands should be placed slightly above the positions corresponding to 9 o'clock and 3 o'clock (see *a*, in fig. 5). In this attitude the arm muscles exert the maximum force with the maximum of precision. I advise this position, *a*, even while cornering.

To take a corner these are the movements that should be followed (see fig. 5), given a right-hand corner requiring the steering-wheel to be turned through almost 90°. Just before entering the corner, transfer the grip of the right hand from the '3 o'clock' position to '1 o'clock' (*c–d* in fig. 5). At the appropriate moment let the right arm turn the wheel clockwise to the extent required (i.e. in this case nearly 90°). The left hand, relaxing its grip, lets the wheel run through the required angle; then, when the right arm has done its stuff, the left re-tightens its grip. Note that the hand has not

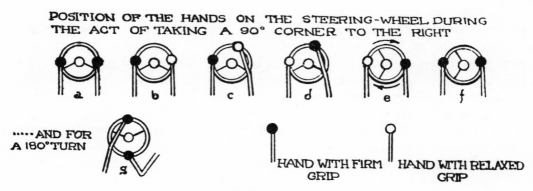

POSITION OF THE HANDS ON THE STEERING-WHEEL DURING THE ACT OF TAKING A 90° CORNER TO THE RIGHT

a   b   c   d   e   f

·····AND FOR A 180° TURN   g

HAND WITH FIRM GRIP   HAND WITH RELAXED GRIP

FIG 5

changed its position, but the rim has moved through 90° (*e–f* in fig. 5). From here the movement can be increased to 180° (*g* in fig. 5).

To straighten up, these movements are repeated in the reverse direction; however, most cars are designed with some self-centering action, and in practice it is often enough to relax both hands slightly and allow the wheel to spin back to position *a*.

When it is necessary to take corners (e.g. hairpin bends) that require more than half a turn of the steering-wheel, the technique is to repeat the above series of operations as often as necessary, so that you arrive at the centre of the corner with the hands in the approved position and, if possible, *not* with the arms crossed as in fig. 6. In this position the hands cannot have

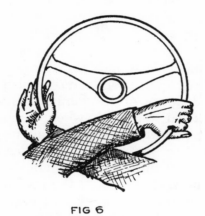

FIG 6

effective and precise control of the wheel. In racing cars with fairly 'direct' steering, even hairpin bends can often be taken with only one displacement of the hands.

ACCESSIBILITY OF THE CONTROLS AND VIEW OF THE ROAD From the driving seat you should be able to reach and move every control with the maximum dispatch. You should sit at the correct distance from the pedals, in such a way that when you straighten your leg the pedal goes all the way down. The position of brake and accelerator pedals is very important, both as regards their direction of travel and their relation to one another: they should be so placed that you can work one with the heel and the other with the toe of the same foot when it is necessary to brake and change down at the same time.

Above all, you should have a good view of the road and, if possible, of the wheels as well, because there will be moments, especially while cornering, when you will want to place them as near as you can to the edge of the road. The faster lap times made by racing cars, as opposed to sports cars, on twisty circuits are partly due to this better visibility. On sports and touring cars, however, in which the driver sits to one side, the near-side front part of the car is completely hidden, and when cornering in this direction you must act largely by guesswork. You have to learn, therefore, to calculate the exact distance that separates the piece of wing that you can see from the point where the tyre touches the road.

A very low driving seat does not make for good visibility, although it can be an advantage, especially in open cars, both aerodynamically and because it lowers the driver's centre of gravity. On winding circuits, where the aerodynamic factor is negligible, it is better to sit up rather high, so that you can see the shape of the bonnet and can 'place' the front wheels on the exact line. This high seating position also allows corners to be seen in perspective, which can be very helpful on unfamiliar circuits.

With open cars, much thought is always given to the height and shape of the windscreen. My advice is to look over the top of the screen, because the glass always gets dirty after a while and spoils one's view of the road. On closed cars a wind-deflector on the bonnet has been tried with success and it keeps the screen clear, especially when the air is filled with midges. This device lightens the task of the windscreen-wiper when it rains and is useful on very fast cars. A second wiper is advised in case the first one goes wrong. Races have been lost through wipers not working properly!

I recommend keeping a close eye on the instruments, particularly the revolution counter and oil-pressure gauge, as these show the state of the engine's health. Make sure that the spokes of the steering-wheel do not hide these dials in the straight-ahead position. It is a good idea to paint a red line at the point which the needle must not pass if the motor is to remain in one piece. Before the start of a race, particularly in a strange car, memorize the position of the most important instruments. You will not have much time for reading, so you must be able to take things in at a glance.

Not enough attention is given to driving-positions by the people who manufacture and prepare racing cars, because they are too busy thinking about the engine and chassis. I am convinced that if they gave proper thought to these matters they would often get better results from their cars and drivers.

4

THE START · CHANGING UP · DRIVING ON THE STRAIGHT

VARIOUS TYPES of starting procedure are used in motor racing. At hill-climbs and in road events like the Mille Miglia, the driver is sent off by himself. In circuit racing, the cars are generally drawn up on a grid, with engines running in an order based on practice times. The starting signal is given by a flag, or, sometimes, by 'traffic lights'. Numbered boards are held up to show how many minutes remain before the 'off'.

The deafening noise of the engines, and the cotton-wool or special wax ear-plugs that drivers use, make it difficult to keep the revs. under control, especially as one eye is busy watching the starter's flag, while the other, as it were, is plotting possible ways to weave past the other cars. So be careful; a lot of drivers (and good ones at that, if a bit over-anxious) have been left sitting on the line with a broken transmission or wrecked engine! A valve-spring, for example, can easily break if the revs. are allowed to rise past the danger-mark.

At Le Mans and other sports car races, another system is used: the cars are lined up on one side of the road and the drivers on the other. As the flag falls they have to run across, jump in, and start by means of the starter. Naturally the car is already in gear and the ignition switched on. The driver just puts the clutch out, presses the button, and . . . away!

At Indianapolis, and in certain other rare cases, they use a rolling start behind a 'pace car'. Lined up in predetermined order, the cars do a relatively slow lap in formation, then the pace car draws to one side, letting the racers sweep past.

A good start is of the highest importance; don't 'start in top gear', as the saying goes, but in first! On a crowded grid a bad get-away can mean the loss of many seconds, including much time spent later in passing slower cars whose drivers made a better start.

The maximum acceleration of a vehicle is obtained when the driving wheels have fed into them the maximum torque produced by the engine; and this force is obviously greatest, thanks to the multiplication of the transmission system, in the lowest gear. The application of this force, however, which has to reach the road via the tyres before it can accelerate the car, is limited by the co-efficient of adhesion existing between the tyres and the road. The value of this force is obtained by multiplying the weight that bears upon the driving wheels by the co-efficient of adhesion between the tyres and the road. This co-efficient reaches its highest value when the wheels are rolling; there is a sharp drop, however, the moment the wheels are allowed to spin much, and if wheelspin is complete the co-efficient of adhesion becomes a co-efficient of friction, assuming a lower value. It is therefore enormously important to know, and to be able to assess, the adhesion factor of a given road surface. At the start of a race you should exploit this factor to the full, while taking care not to spin the wheels wildly, because when they are spinning the co-efficient of friction reaches values that are, especially in the wet, inferior to the co-efficient of adhesion. It follows that the acceleration of the car will suffer.

To get the most out of your machine, and thus be able to make perfect get-aways, it is well to be familiar with the 'characteristic performance curves' of the engine (see fig. 7) or at any rate the revs. at which it gives maximum power, and the rev.-limit that must not be exceeded, which in a robustly constructed engine will generally be somewhat higher. The mechanic who has worked on the engine can give useful advice on this subject. Manufacturers show the safe rev.-limit by painting a red line, or better still a red sector, on the dial of the rev.-counter. To ignore this is looking for trouble, which will arrive all the sooner and more expensively the more highly tuned the engine is. It is essential to acquire a very light and sensitive touch on the clutch pedal, and to know exactly how resistant the clutch is to 'slip'.

CHANGING UP On touring cars, which are generally fairly heavy for their low power and fitted with good strong clutches and clutch-linings that take up the drive progressively, the 'take-off' is relatively simple. In contrast to a normal 'touring' start, the revs. are taken fairly high—certainly above the speed giving maximum torque—before the pedal is released. Do this at the last moment, and not some while before as I have often heard novices and wild men do. Once you are 'off', hold the clutch at slipping point until the car has reached 30–50 per cent of its maximum speed in bottom gear. To get the best out of this initial period, you have to put your foot hard down at the moment of starting, and play skilfully with the clutch in such a way that its limited slip will just allow the engine to maintain the proper number of revolutions, i.e. between maximum torque and maximum power. After this initial 'clutch-slip phase' you proceed in the

III.

Above: Taruffi in a 3300 Lancia sports car at the start of the 9th Catania-Etna, which he won in 1954. Notice the leather eye-shield to prevent dazzle and the chamois-leather backs to the gloves, used for wiping goggles.

Below: Von Trips and Luigi Musso use the all-round type of visor for racing in the wet. The event is the 1958 G.P. of Buenos Aires.

IV.

Above: The author after winning the Mille Miglia in 1957. Note what he is wearing: light lace-up boots, trousers with pockets on top of the thighs and above the knee, and a woollen jersey with just the upper part and the arms made of waterproof material.

Below: Jimmy Bryan, who won the 500 miles of Monza in 1957 and the Indianapolis 500 in 1958, wears a shoulder-harness to keep him in the driving seat. Notice also the American type of crash helmet, which fits down over the ears.

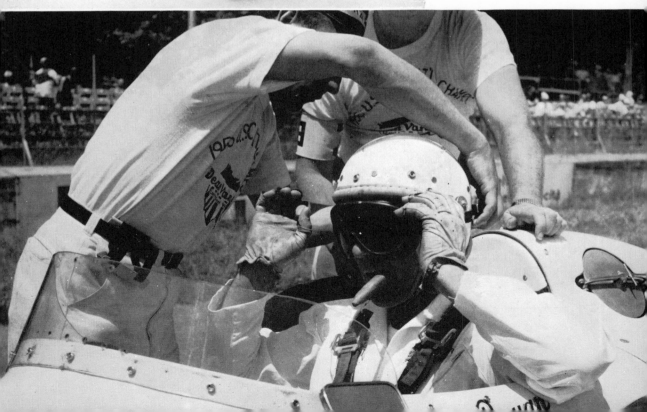

V. *Above:* To prevent yourself being thrown about by bumps and by centrifugal force, plant your left foot firmly on the floor.

Below: The arms should be almost straight.

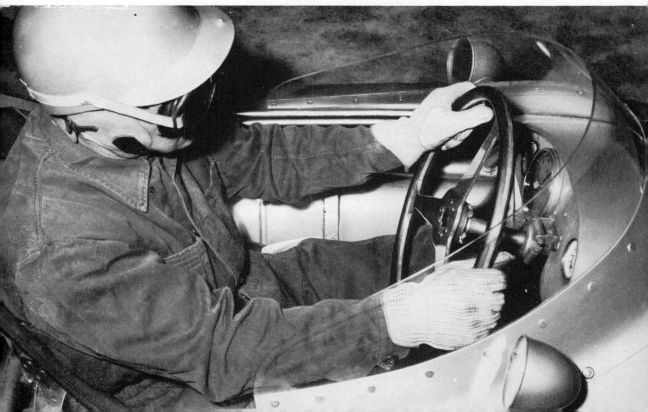

VI.
Turning the wheel
through 180°: three men
on the same corner—
101 Ascari, 102 Farina,
103 Taruffi with Ferraris
on the Nurburgring.

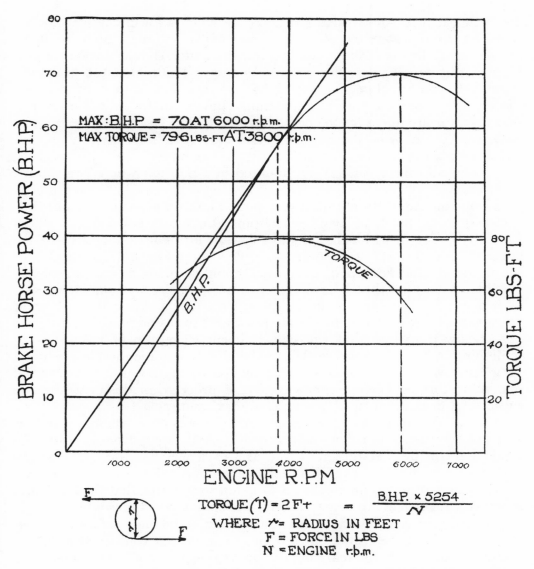

Fig. 7 details:

BRAKE HORSE POWER (B.H.P.)

ENGINE R.P.M

TORQUE LBS-FT

MAX: B.H.P. = 70 AT 6000 r.p.m.
MAX TORQUE = 79·6 LBS-FT AT 3800 r.p.m.

B.H.P.

TORQUE

$$\text{TORQUE}\,(T) = 2F\,r = \frac{\text{B.H.P.} \times 5254}{N}$$

WHERE r = RADIUS IN FEET
F = FORCE IN LBS
N = ENGINE r.p.m.

CHARACTERISTIC POWER CURVES
FIG 7

normal way, keeping your foot down until the engine reaches maximum-power revs. in first gear. Then you change up, doing this as expeditiously as possible, though without risking a breakage in the transmission. If the latter is sufficiently robust you may be able to change without even lifting your accelerator foot. Such methods should not be abused, however, and they are better kept for short races and those in which a lot of changes are not required. If repeated too often they may burn out the clutch lining by over-heating. In the ensuing changes up, the clutch should not be slipped, because this causes a needless waste of energy. The higher the gear-ratio into which you are changing, the higher the revs. should be carried before the change: from the speed of maximum power up towards the limit of safety. Naturally this is for 'record' take-offs. Unless you have an especially well trained ear, you should keep inside the rev. limit by timing your changes by a speedometer, or better still a rev.-counter. These instruments, more than all others, should be mounted in a position where you can see them easily.

In making rapid starts with a very potent lightweight car, much greater care has to be taken to avoid wheelspin. On this sort of car the clutch generally comes in with a bang, and this calls for delicate footwork. If the engine accelerates well from low revs., it does not do to prolong the clutch-slip in the manner described; the clutch should be made to 'bite' as soon as possible. A method that I have found to answer very well on racing cars with a low bottom gear is the following: start by holding the engine at 30–50 per cent revs., let in the clutch quickly, at the same time dropping the revs. below the speed that will cause violent wheelspin or risk breaking something in the transmission. When the clutch is home, accelerate again progressively for a few yards, without necessarily getting up to the revs. of maximum torque. Change into second and proceed, in this gear and the succeeding ones, right up to the revs. of maximum power.

Repeated rehearsals of the racing start are not to be recommended, as you run the risk of burning out the clutch. And, apart from limiting the number of racing take-offs, it is well also to space them out, so that the clutch has a chance to cool off between one attempt and the next. Sometimes people worry so much about their starts during practice that the car is not fit to race. A smell of burning is a useful warning of possible trouble.

On the grid you should get into gear about 10 seconds before the start, so as not to hold the clutch out too long: you do not want to tire the leg muscles so that when the real moment comes they will not have the delicacy of control required for the act of starting. If the clutch does not free properly, do not hold the car on the hand-brake; a little stone placed in front of one of the front wheels will do the trick, and there is one less thing to do as the flag falls.

Generally, engines are started one minute before the flag; to do so much before, in a car not fitted with a fan, is to run the risk of boiling.

It is a good thing to know when there are 20 and then 5 seconds to go before the start: during the first 15 you put on your goggles and get into gear, leaving the remaining 5 to get set for the 'off'. If these warnings are not given by the organizers, you can supply them yourself by having a stopwatch on board, or you can arrange for signals from a friend.

At a hill-climb, start concentrating at once; you can win by a fraction of a second. Here it is a case of 'straight-through' changes—just the opposite of a long-distance event, in which the clutch and gearbox might not stand up to such treatment.

In massed starts, try as far as possible to avoid wandering from the straight line, so that you do not get 'shunted' by other competitors, and if you have not taken the lead remember that the first corners in a race are the most dangerous and the ones where accidents are most likely to occur.

DRIVING ON THE STRAIGHT   As the speed builds up you must take increasing care with your driving. Keep in mind that any unnecessary movement of the steering, any change of direction imparted to the vehicle, is wasting energy at a rate proportional to the square of the speed; and it is the same with your bodily strength. On the straight you can rest the arm muscles after their work on the corners. They can now relax, although always on the alert.

On this part of the course, too, you can look to the health of your engine: observe the oil-pressure, the water temperature, the revs. it is pulling at the end of the longest straight. During practice this tells you whether the car has been well prepared, and in the race itself it can save you from costly blow-ups.

Try to plot the course that is shortest, and where the road surface is best and most inviting.

If there is a strong cross wind, hug the windward side of the road and you will have the camber of the road in your favour as well; try however not to baulk a competitor wishing to overtake. Pay special attention when running close to buildings, and where the road has been repaired. As you emerge from shelter, try and anticipate the gust of wind.

If you are not one of the fastest, keep as far to the right-hand side as possible and keep an eye on the rear-view mirror. Baulking is one of the recognized crimes.

The moment another car passes you, if the difference in speed is not too great, try and tuck in behind it, and get the benefit of a 'tow'. Slipstreaming can add quite a bit to your speed. The closer you can manage to stay to the car in front, the greater the advantage you get. Caution: this needs a certain amount of experience. The advantage of slipstreaming is greatest at high speeds, and it varies as the square of the speed. Below 60 m.p.h. the saving is negligible.

Take special care, though, when slowing down. The distance between cars in a race is measured not in yards but in seconds; this means that if two cars are lapping at the same average speed the *time* interval between them remains constant. On the straight a speed of 110 m.p.h. means 160 feet per sec., and 32 feet covered represents one-fifth of a second. If the time interval remains unchanged while the cars go into a hairpin bend which can be taken at 25 m.p.h. (i.e. 37 feet per sec.) the 32 feet will shrink to 7·5, and the man behind, for all that he has gained nothing, may ram the leading car in the tail. The 32 feet interval will re-establish itself on the next straight when the cars get back to their 110 m.p.h.

Through this difference, which is apparent rather than real, spectators often quite wrongly conclude that the man behind is the better driver and that the leading car has better acceleration. Simply by reason of the way this distance varies, cars often shunt one another from behind. This happens most frequently on very slow corners.

Some drivers, when overtaken on the straight some few hundred yards after a bend, are apt to think that their car is slower than their rival's, even though an identical model. It may be that there is some difference in performance between the two machines, but it is much more likely that the overtaking driver managed to come out of the last corner at a higher speed.

If a straight is several miles long and you are driving in a race lasting many hours, it is a good idea to 'lift your foot' slightly every half mile or so if you are dubious about the durability of your engine; the time lost will be negligible.

The higher the speed, the greater attention you should pay. The moments that you can spare to glance away from the road are exceedingly brief. Do not turn round to see what is coming behind, but use the mirror, and make sure *personally* that it is clean and properly adjusted beforehand, in practice, not just as the race is starting. Turning round, even to read a pit-signal, can lead to involuntary movements of the wheel, and hence to snaking, which can be a menace to all.

If you wish to leave your usual 'line' during a race, or to slow down, as will happen before a call at the pits, you must make sure that you are not inconveniencing people behind, and you must signal your intention in good time with a wave of your arm. Accidents have occurred through people omitting to do this.

If you are driving down a straight that includes what I call 'vertical curves', such as humps, bridges, culverts or gulleys, you must use a certain amount of judgment. If you give a slight touch of brake as you arrive on top of a hump, this will be ironed out better, and the car will not jump so far for a given speed. If you are going so fast that the car actually leaves the ground, remember that such things as weight distribution and aerodynamic shape may cause the car to change its attitude while in the air, so that it is no longer perfectly horizontal. From the control point of view, it is preferable that the rear wheels should strike the ground first, if only by a little.

You are not quite helpless about the attitude your car will assume while in the air. It will tend to 'nose dive' or come down tail-first according to whether you lifted your foot or accelerated just before the take-off. In any case you must not accelerate while in the air, for fear of over-revving the engine, and of breaking something or setting-up wheelspin when you land. When going really fast, it is essential to come down absolutely straight, so watch out if there is a wind! The car may be blown off course while in the air.

In long-distance road races, like the Mille Miglia, 'vertical curves' can represent an unknown factor, because they are difficult to judge at first sight. Look out for yourself and for your car, especially if fully loaded; it is better to lift your foot once too often than to do so once too seldom!

On the Continent there are often wide gulleys where watercourses cross the road; these require care. If the gulley is short and its edges are well 'faired in' to the road each side, and especially if it lies on a downhill stretch with its farther edge at a lower level than that nearest you, you can try taking it flat out; at high speed the wheels, by reason of their inertia, will not have time to come down after leaving the near-side edge of the gulley, and will renew contact with the farther edge almost without a jar. In this this case the depth of the gulley does not count. But you have got to take it very fast, and very decisively. Should you come upon it at moderate speed, however, it is best to slow down even more, depending upon the depth. If the depression is several yards wide, and quite deep, you should bring your speed right down, because, if the car is going too fast when it comes out on the far side, the suspension may 'bottom' and come to grief.

5

SLOWING DOWN · BRAKING · CHANGING TO A LOWER GEAR

IF YOU merely wish to slow down it suffices to close the throttle; if quicker deceleration is required, you must use the brakes on the wheels. Closing the throttle takes advantage, through the gearbox, of the internal resistance of the engine, which is communicated to the driving wheels. The faster the engine is turning, the greater this resistance will be; that is why drivers come down through the box, using each gear in succession. This does not shorten the theoretical stopping-distance of the car, but it does lighten the work of the brakes.

The car slows under the brakes in a degree proportional to the square of the speed and of the wind resistance. So-called 'aerodynamic' cars require a longer braking distance, for a given speed, than cars of less streamlined shape. Drivers of this sort of car must bear this in mind, especially when braking from high speed.

As regards the retarding effect of the brakes on the wheels, this is based solely upon the force of adhesion between the vehicle and the road, this force being proportional, as we have already seen, to the weight of the car and the co-efficient of adhesion between its tyres and the road. It is extremely important, therefore, to know, and to be able to assess, the state of the road surface.

The retarding force acting throughout the whole braking period is the force which opposes the car's forward motion, counteracting the kinetic energy stored up by the vehicle, which is directly proportional to the weight of the vehicle and the square of its speed.

If now other forces are applied to the wheels, as, for example, the centrifugal force generated by cornering, the braking force will combine with this to give a resultant which cannot be greater than the force of adhesion between the wheels and the road, which, before the intervention of the centrifugal force, was completely available for slowing the vehicle. As it is now only partly so, the braking action is reduced.

It must also be borne in mind that the centrifugal force in cornering, which acts through the centre of gravity of the car and thus at a certain height from the ground, causes a transfer of weight from the inside wheels to those on the outside, so that the former are lightened and have less adhesion. If you do not reduce your pressure on the brake pedal, the wheel that has the smallest force pressing it down will eventually lock, and the stability of the car will be seriously affected.

The occasion which calls for the greatest care is when the brakes have to be applied while cornering downhill. In this case it is the inside rear wheel which locks first, and causes the rear end of the car to 'break away'. If you have already turned the front wheels as you brake for a hairpin bend, these are the first to lock, and the car tends to go straight on; fortunately in this case the speed is pretty low.

For these reasons, avoid braking on corners: it is less effective, and may be dangerous.

The same principle applies in braking as that which we discussed under the heading of acceleration: there must be no slippage between tyre and road. Should a point be reached where one or more wheels lock under braking, the stopping distance of the car is increased, and control may be affected.

BRAKING DISTANCES Knowing the speed and the co-efficient of adhesion between tyres and road, we can calculate the stopping distance for any car by means of a simple formula derived from the above considerations:

$$S = \frac{V^2}{64f}$$

where S is the stopping distance in feet,
  V is the speed of the vehicle in feet per second,
  f is the co-efficient of adhesion between tyres and road,
  64 is an approximation to $64 \cdot 4 = 2 \times 32 \cdot 2 = 2 \times g$
   (g being the acceleration due to gravity)
   (expressed as feet per second per second)

You will see from this formula that braking distance is not, as many people imagine, influenced by the weight of the car.

For convenience we print a table giving values for the co-efficient of adhesion, and a graph showing stopping distances for vehicles with brakes on all four wheels, acting with an efficiency of 100 per cent, and travelling at speeds between 0 and 200 m.p.h. on roads whose co-efficient varies between ·1 and ·8. In these tables no account is taken of the driver's 'reaction time' (see fig. 8), or fall off of efficiency arising from the heating up of the brake linings.

CO-EFFICIENTS OF ADHESION BETWEEN TYRE AND ROAD

Type of Surface Dressing				Dry	Wet
Tarred macadam	..	..	..	·8	·55
Rough concrete ..	..	..	..	·8	·55
Smooth asphalt ..	..	..	..	·7	·4
Cobblestones (pavé)	..	..	..	·6	·4
Wood blocks	..	..	..	·6	·3
Snow	..	..	..	—	·2 to ·15
Ice	..	..	..	—	·1 to ·05

These co-efficients are approximate and may vary by + or − 10 per cent, depending on road conditions, the design of tyre treads and the type of 'mix' used in their construction. On wet roads, for example, the co-efficients increase by ·1 if the tyres are 'cut', and decrease sharply if they are smooth. They also diminish slightly with a rise in speed.

From this graph we can calculate, by noting the difference in feet, the distance required to slow from a speed of X to a speed of Y. In practice these figures should be approached in easy stages, preferably on a circuit that can be lapped repeatedly, by decreasing gradually the braking distance before each corner. Having reached the optimum result, it is a good plan to mark the cut-off point in your mind with some object—a tree, a house, etc.; but do choose a mark that cannot be moved! Boards are often erected for the assistance of drivers before corners that come at the end of a long straight, marked 300—200—100, this being the distance in yards between the board and the start of the corner itself.

It is a good thing, however, for every driver to train himself to judge speeds and distances accurately by eye. This is an immensely valuable faculty and absolutely essential for anyone taking up racing.

Without going into the technical details of brake design, I think I should here make plain that these components, as they are used in racing, are not inexhaustible either in life or efficiency. It is a driver's job, therefore, to discover the precise capacity of his brakes, remembering that the result of a race may sometimes hang upon whether or not he has been sensible and used them with discretion. This applies particularly in long-distance races where, from the nature of the course, the car has to be slowed from very high to quite low speeds. In these conditions, and with certain types of brakes, serious overheating may occur, with rapid wear on the linings.

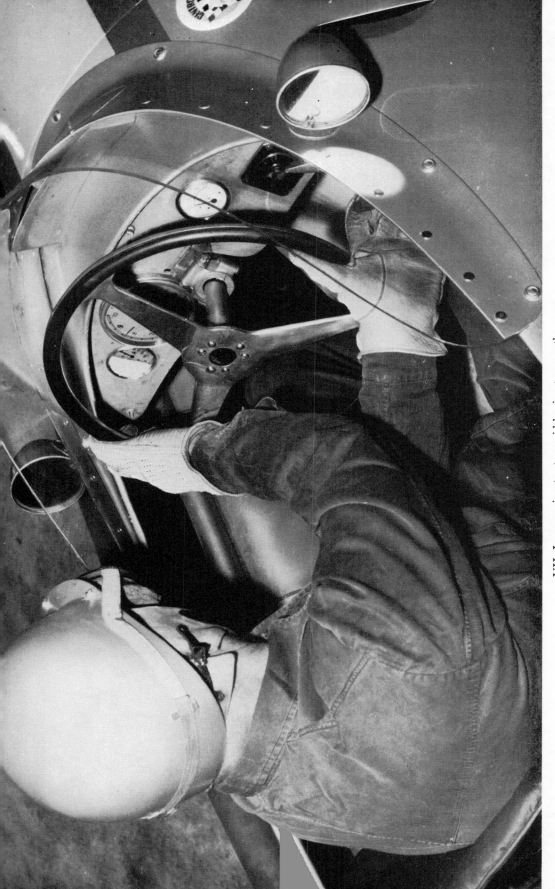

VII. In cornering try to avoid having to cross the arms.

VIII. *Above:* 'Five seconds to go!' The author starting in the Mille Miglia of 1957. Cars are dispatched one at a time from a raised starting ramp. In this picture can be seen, from left to right: Count Aymo Maggi, Signor Boni, Mayor of Brescia, Signora Taruffi—waiting to let fall the starter's flag while Renzo Castagneto looks over her shoulder, and a timekeeper ticks off the seconds with his hand.

Below: The line-up for the start at Modena. Grid positions are allotted on the best lap times recorded in practice.

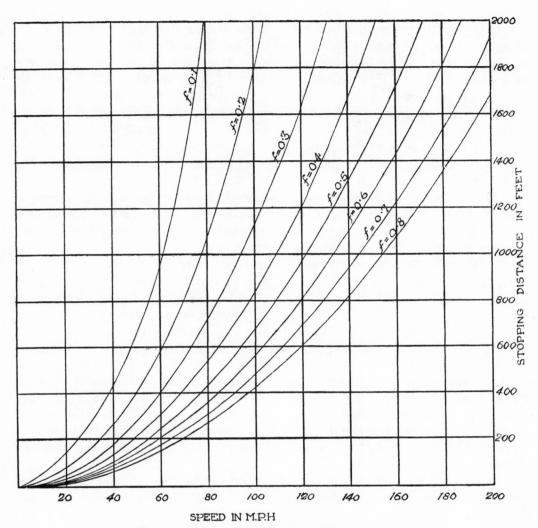

THEORETICAL STOPPING DISTANCE
FIG 8

As a result of overheating, the brakes may lose their efficiency towards the end of an application because the co-efficient of friction of the linings has diminished, in which case the braking distance allowed may prove to be insufficient. Worn linings are more or less bound to entail a stop at the pits for adjustment, with a consequent loss of time.

Here is a way of keeping heat within bounds. Suppose you are driving flat-out in fourth gear: close the throttle and allow the car to slow for a certain distance simply by the pressure of the wind and the braking effect of

33

the engine. Then press the brake to reduce your speed enough to permit a change into the next lowest gear, in this case third. Release the brake for a while and once again rely simply on the over-run. When the speed has fallen substantially, there comes a moment, which only personal experience of your brakes can tell you, when you should tread on the brakes really hard, and continue braking while you change into second and then into bottom, if that gear is required for the corner. The idea is to take advantage, during the initial stage, of wind-resistance, which is greatest at high speed, and save the wheel-brakes for the second, low-speed phase of the operation. How far to apply this system, and how often, will depend on the type, number and spacing of the places where brakes are needed on a given circuit. Enough time should be allowed after each application for the brakes to cool off, exactly how long depending upon the amount of kinetic energy that had to be disposed after the last brake application.

At Sebring (see page 117) for instance, it is usual, in the majority of cars, to apply this method, especially on arriving at Curve 11, which comes at the end of the longest straight, and before a second long straight leading to Corner 12. If the system has been properly used on number 11, the brakes will still retain their power at number 12. Elsewhere on this circuit the brakes may be used hard and continuously. Similar examples can be found on every course, and it is up to the driver to apply the proper treatment.

On cars where the brakes are too small or inefficiently cooled, it is a good idea to brake in a series of jabs, allowing short rests between, during which the linings are cooled by the momentarily improved circulation of air between themselves and the drum. When, however, there is no doubt about their efficacy, the brakes are used without respite; that is the way to slow down in the shortest distance.

To reduce the consumption of brake-linings, you should never let them overheat. Try to avoid high specific pressures on the linings by never pushing the pedal with sudden violence, and spare them as much as possible by letting the gearbox do some of the work. When it rains, the brakes have an easier time; make sure, though, that arrangements designed to assist brake cooling do not let water get on the linings, as this will momentarily reduce their co-efficient of friction.

During the lighter braking that is necessary on slippery road surfaces, remember that less weight will be thrown upon the front wheels and the brakes on these wheels may therefore be more apt to lock.

CHANGING DOWN This operation takes place either while slowing up or, on machines of low power, when the engine starts to flag on a hill.

There are two ways of changing: in the first you press the clutch pedal, move the gear lever into neutral, then engage the lower gear, accelerating slightly and gently letting in the clutch. This method works quickly and well on cars with a syncro-mesh box, and if the ratios are fairly close one can change down on the over-run without even accelerating.

The second method is that known as 'double-declutching'. In this method you depress the clutch, move the lever into neutral and let the clutch 'in' again for a moment, at the same time using the accelerator. The clutch is then pressed down, the lower gear engaged, and the clutch pedal released. At this point you should accelerate hard if the object is hill-climbing, but close the throttle if you wish to slow down. This manœuvre sounds more complicated than it is, and after a little practice one does it automatically.

Double-declutching is recommended when gears are difficult to change. If done properly it is not so apt to cause wheelspin as the other method, and the gearbox and transmission suffer less strain. Double-declutching, there-fore, is most advisable, and every sporting driver should be able to do it.

To know what revs. to change down at, so as to obtain most benefit from the braking effect of the engine, let us take an example. Suppose that the gearbox ratios on your car are 1:1 in fourth or top, 1·2:1 in third, 1·5:1 in second, and 2:1 in first, and that the safe rev.-limit is 5,000 r.p.m. In changing up it is easy, if a rev.-counter is fitted, to observe how many revs. the engine 'drops' as you change from a low gear to a higher one after going up to maximum revs. With the ratios cited above, if you have gone up to 5,000 in third you will see the needle swing back to 4,170 as you change into top $(5,000 : \frac{1·0}{1·2})$, to 4,000 $(5,000 : \frac{1·2}{1·5})$ when changing from second to third, and so on. The converse will happen when you change from a high gear to a lower one. To be sure, therefore, that you will not over-rev., stay in top until the engine speed has fallen to at least 4,170 on the over-run before going into third, in third until 4,000, in second until 3,760. A maximum-reading hand on the rev.-counter—Italian drivers call it a 'spy'!—can be useful in recording those mistakes that in practice are so easily made.

When you are braking and wish to change down as well, there is a technique known as 'heeling-and-toeing'. The toe of the foot is used on the brake and the heel on the accelerator. For this to succeed, the relative positions of the pedals must have been carefully arranged, otherwise it is not possible to exert a strong yet perfectly controlled pressure on the brake.

The brake pedal may be placed either in the centre or on the right. In the first case, which is the more usual, you turn the toe of your foot to the left, thus getting into a rather unnatural position as shown in fig. 9. To make up for this, however, your right leg, which is the outside one, can exert a more controlled pressure on the accelerator because you can brace it against the side of the body.

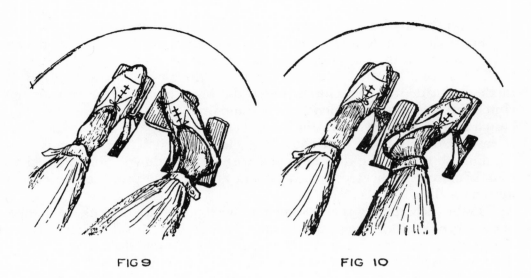

FIG 9   FIG 10

With a central accelerator, the leg assumes a more natural position, as shown in fig. 10. One has to be very careful, when swopping about from one car to another, not to press the accelerator instead of the brake!

Only in very rare cases does one have to change directly from the high gear used on the straight into the low one required by a corner, omitting a gear in between (e.g., from fourth to second, or from top direct into bottom). This may slightly shorten the braking distance if the efficiency and adjustment of the brakes are perfect. I have done it occasionally in hill-climbs when arriving at a hairpin too late—and too fast—to do anything else. With this method indeed, although it needs a very good ear to judge the change correctly, you have the advantage that the brake pedal is continuously pressed to the limit, and you can keep both hands on the wheel, except when making this single gear-change; and in a really frenzied bit of braking, this is no bad thing.

Normally, however, do like other drivers, and go through all the gears. It is not so much strain on the brakes, gear-changing is simplified, and there is less risk of setting up wheelspin through bad synchronization of the speeds of the engine and wheels. However, for reasons which we shall discuss later, you should not change gear while actually cornering.

6

CORNERING

---

1 · *The Conventional 'Line'*

YOU WILL have noticed that the most crowded parts of a circuit are those alongside the corners; these are the most difficult bits and it is here that a front rank driver, no better mounted than his opponents, picks up the time that may win him the race.

You can recognize the best men on a corner by the way in which they keep to precisely the same 'line', lap after lap, and by the way they go round at the limit of adhesion, in a perfectly controlled drift.

If one watches closely there are small differences even amongst the best which distinguish each man's style, and to a certain extent, his character. I would mention two of the greatest Italian champions, who, during the period that they were both racing, represented two different schools: Nuvolari, the dashing master of 'over-the-limit' motoring and Varzi, regular as clockwork, and always perfectly controlled.

People often compare present-day drivers and those of the past. If any difference exists it is due mainly to progress in the design and construction of motor-cars and roads. This progress has tended to iron out inequalities and bring improvements in driving technique; and these in their turn have led to the discovery of new and better design features. The engineer's world and the driver's world have grown closer together. One thing is certain, though: whether we are speaking of yesterday or today the selfsame physical laws hold good. It is essential to understand these laws and how they affect the handling of a car. Once we understand them, we can turn to advantage the factors in our favour, and manage to avoid the others. Let us start by considering:

CENTRIFUGAL FORCE AND THE FORCE OF ADHESION When cornering a car is subjected to two turning moments in the plane of the road: one

37

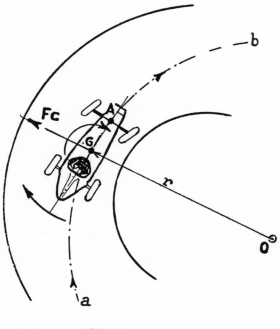

FIG 11

about point O, the centre of the curve being taken (fig. 11), and a second about its own centre of gravity, G.

Taking W to represent the weight of the car expressed in lbs, with r as the distance between G and O, and with V as the velocity in feet per second, the car is subjected, by reason of its rotation about O, to a centrifugal force

$$Fc = \frac{W}{g} \times \frac{V^2}{r}$$

where g = 32·2 (feet per sec.²), the acceleration due to gravity.

By the effect of this force the vehicle would be pushed towards the outside of the corner, were it not for Wf the adhesion of the wheels to the ground, which is proportional to the weight of the car, W, and the co-efficient of adhesion f between the tyres and the road.

Assuming a road surface that is perfectly level, we can work out, as the two forces, centrifugal and adhesional, are equal, the maximum speed at which a car can be thrust through a corner of radius r when no forces other than centrifugal force are acting upon it:

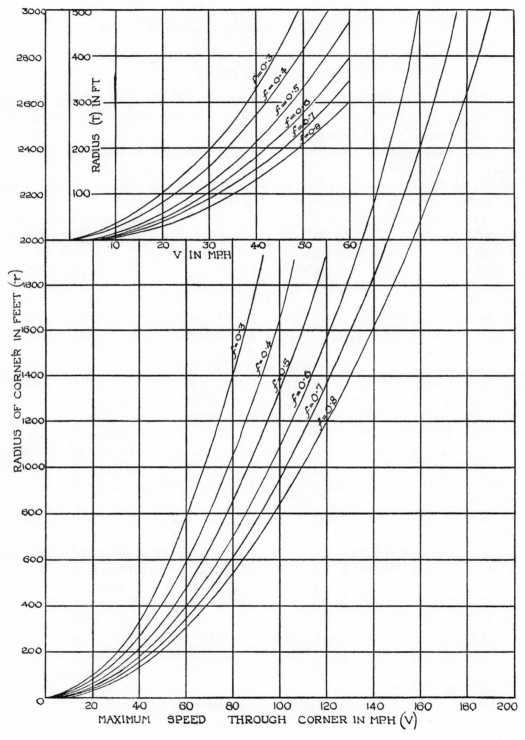

FIG 12

$$Wf = \frac{W}{g} \times \frac{V^2}{r} \text{ so that by simple cross-multiplication}$$

$$V = \sqrt{gfr}, \text{ or approximately} = \sqrt{32fr}.$$

From this last formula we derive the graph in fig. 12, which gives the maximum speed for flat curves up to r = 3,000 feet, given the radius and the co-efficient of adhesion.

The graph shows that the limiting velocity for a curve of 300 feet radius, on a surface of good tarred macadam having a co-efficient of 0·8, is about 60 m.p.h. In order to double this speed, we should have to describe a curve of four times this radius, i.e. 1,200 feet.

The situation with regard to the co-efficient of adhesion is analogous. Should the limit-speed be halved, it would be necessary for the adhesion factor to be reduced to one quarter. Such a reduction, except in very rare cases, does not take place, even when a dry road suddenly gets wet. Modern roads made of concrete or tarred stone-chippings have a dry/wet co-efficient that varies between 0·8 and 0·6 or so. Reference to the graph will show that the reduction in speed due to wet roads does not amount to more than 15–20 per cent. Better adhesion can be obtained by the use of special wet-weather tyres with 'cut' tread pattern.

TYPES OF CORNERS AND THEIR CHARACTERISTICS To help in following the argument concerning the speed at which a corner can be taken, the following seven factors should be borne in mind:

(1) Radius of corner measured along the road axis (2) Arc of curvature (3) Available width of road (4) Co-efficient of adhesion between tyres and road (5) Any 'banking' of the corner (6) Variations of slope in the longitudinal section (e.g., humps and gulleys) (7) camber.

For simplicity let us start by considering only the first four of these elements.

By 'radius of the road axis of the corner' is meant the radius, in feet, of a curved line following the centre of the road—the dotted line in fig. 13.

By 'arc of curvature' is meant the arc, measured in degrees, between the two bordering straights (fig. 14). The length of the inner arc xy, measured in feet, is proportional to the angle, and to the radius of the curve.

The 'available width of the road' is that part of it which a car can drive over in stable fashion, and which possesses a co-efficient of adhesion that is approximately constant. Values for this co-efficient were set out in the chapter on Braking.

It is well first of all to distinguish between what I have called the 'radius

IX.
Drivers ready for their
starting sprint at Rheims.

Rolling start at Indiana-
polis, 1954. The cars are
beginning to string out
after their lap in
formation behind the
pace-car, which has just
pulled on to the in-field
on the right.

X. *Above:* During the Supercortemaggiore G.P. for sports cars at Monza in 1956 number 65 gets the benefit of a tow from Stirling Moss in Maserati number 1.

Below: On a sharp corner in the Circuit of Garda, 1949, Serafini (OSCA 1100) is 'shunted' by Tadini's F2 Ferrari.

XI. *Above:* The leading driver lifts a hand to show that he is about to pull in to the pits.

Below: Piero Taruffi and his Lancia 3300 Sport show what he means by a 'vertical curve' in the Mille Miglia of 1954. All four wheels are off the ground.

XII. Close-up of cornering. Eugenio Castellotti and Luigi Musso have very nearly reached their effective apex or 'clipping point' on Lesmo II, the second half of the double right-angled corner at Monza. Behind them three cars in a group are commencing the same manceuvre, all nicely on the correct line, close to the outside of the road. Behind them at the end of the short straight, two other cars are preparing to do the same—the leader well placed near the outside, the man behind him less so, being about a yard and a half from the edge. In the background four other cars have just come round Lesmo I and are heading for the outside.

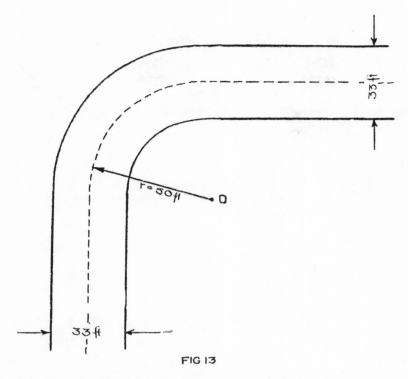

FIG 13

of the road axis' and the actual 'corner' as taken by the car. The former has been defined above; the latter, which could more accurately be called the 'cornering path', conforms in practice to the path taken by the front wheels, assuming that the driver is endeavouring to follow the line he considers best.

In fig. 16, points BC and FC mark the beginning and the end respectively of the curved trajectory or 'corner' described by the car. Lines XX and YY indicate the beginning and the end of the theoretical curve MCR, having the maximum constant radius that can be fitted in to the available road. The point GA at the centre of the corner on the inside is the 'geometrical apex', the point Z is the 'effective apex', which should be clipped by the inside front wheel of the car when taking the best line through the corner.

For simplicity's sake, all paths are drawn as a single line. This corresponds actually to the path described by a vehicle with zero track, like a motor-cycle. For four-wheelers it should really be replaced by two parallel lines corresponding to the wheel marks, and separated by the width of the car's track; the radius of the curve followed would thus be shortened and the speed therefore reduced, but the principle remains unchanged.

To illustrate most of my examples I have chosen a right-angled corner. This one and the others are assumed to be perfectly flat, with a road width

41

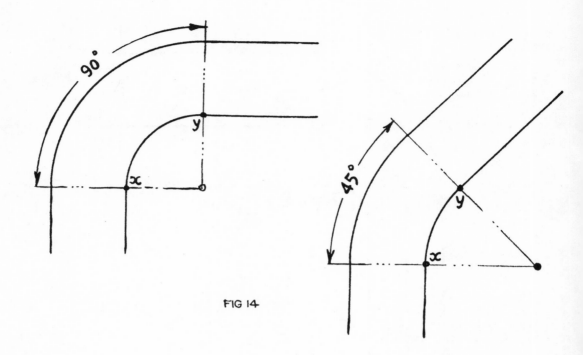

FIG 14

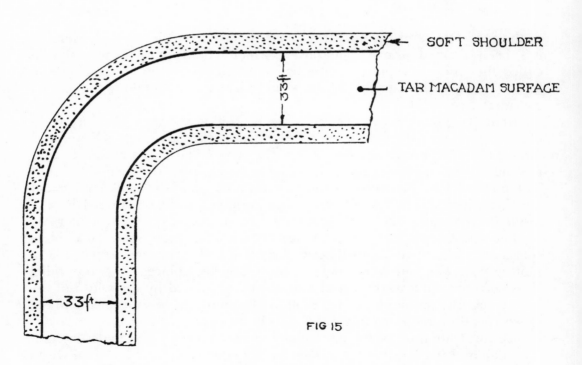

SOFT SHOULDER

TAR MACADAM SURFACE

FIG 15

of 33 feet and an adhesion-factor of f = ·8. The ideas set out can be generally applied.

THE 'CURVE OF MAXIMUM CONSTANT RADIUS'   The formula for speed $V = \sqrt{32ft}$ shows how the speed of a corner is governed, apart from the adhesion-factor, by the radius of the curve described. Therefore, to obtain the utmost speed, you have to describe a curve having a radius as long, and as constant, as the roadway will permit. The length of this radius is governed by the available width of the road, which is wider than the wheel-track of the car; its 'constancy' will depend upon your personal ability to follow a set path, and to hold it without continual changes of radius.

Looking at fig. 16, we see that this path does not follow the 'touring' line T, which keeps well to the right of the central dotted line like a good little continental motorist; it takes the line MCR with centre O and greatly increased radius.

To follow this new 'line', you have to pull well over to the outside before the corner, trying to keep as close to the verge as possible. At the point BC you will start taking the corner in such a way as to clip the inside of it at precisely the half-way mark, i.e. at the geometrical apex GA, and will finish on the extreme outside of the road, at FC.

This path, if followed with a constant radius, has the longest radius that can be fitted into the available road, and is the one which permits the highest speed. In the case illustrated, the course T is some 5 per cent shorter than MCR, but the longer radius of the latter gives a theoretical maximum speed more than double that of T and is therefore incontestably better in terms of time taken to cover the stretch of road. As we shall see in a minute, the maximum-constant-radius course shown in fig. 16 can seldom be realized in practice, and it is only in this special case that the references BC/XX, FC/YY, GA/Z happen to coincide; but we shall refer to it from time to time as an ideal datum-line with which to compare the slightly modified cornering tactics that we shall have to consider.

IMPORTANCE OF DESCRIBING THE 'CURVE OF MAXIMUM CONSTANT RADIUS'   With the aid of the graph in fig. 12, 'Speed on Flat Corners', and the formula $V = \sqrt{32ft}$, you will see how very much faster it is to follow the path of maximum radius B in fig. 17 instead of line A. This difference shows up equally in practice. If the road has a co-efficient of f = ·8 the difference is about 16 m.p.h. because the limiting speed for line A (the dotted line in the middle, with centre O and radius 50 feet) is 25 m.p.h. while line B (the solid one with centre O' and radius 138 feet) permits 41 m.p.h.

If, instead, you were to enter and leave the corner with one yard between your car and the outside edge of the roadway, while still passing

43

through the mid point GA, you would describe path C (the dotted line with centre O''). This has a smaller radius: 126·5 instead of 138 feet—a reduction which lowers the speed by about 2 m.p.h., because the speed for a radius of r = 126·5 is only 39 m.p.h. This is a difference of almost 5 per cent —more than enough to distinguish a first class driver's performance from that of lesser men.

Figures for cornering speeds quoted in these and succeeding examples

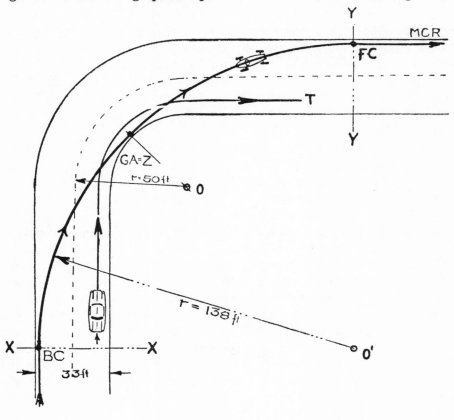

FIG 16

are approximate, and are put in to give a numerical idea of how choosing a different sort of 'line' can affect your speed.

Should you also make the mistake of steering one yard wide of the mid-point GA, (the dotted-and-solid line D having centre O'') the radius falls to 118 feet and the speed to 37 m.p.h.

Even worse results are obtained if, trying to follow the line MCR (see fig. 18), you keep swinging on and off it in a series of continual corrections. You end by taking not one 'corner' of constant and maximum radius, but a succession of curves and counter-curves each of which has a radius far less than the ideal MCR.

This mistake, illustrated (in greatly exaggerated form) in fig. 18, is mainly one of inexperience, but better drivers sometimes fall into it when they meet an unfamiliar and deceptive corner on the road. If the driver

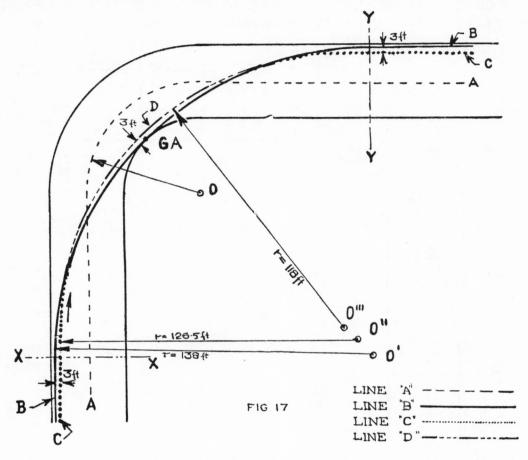

FIG 17

LINE 'A'	– – – – – –
LINE 'B'	———————
LINE 'C'	····················
LINE 'D'	—·—··—··—··

goes in at a speed approaching the limit imposed by MCR, he will end up in a series of skids and slides which, should they become too pronounced, may send him completely out of control.

If you watch the drivers on a circuit, when all of them know the course and each is attaining his own personal limit, you will see that some of them keep at a certain distance from the outside edge of the road, not bothering much about how they go into and come out of a corner. This is one of the more common mistakes. They are much more careful about clipping the apex and, if you examine the roadside afterwards, you may find that where they

45

have gone on the grass this is flattened for a distance of a few inches only.

When, moreover, the verge is on a level or nearly on a level with the tarmac, some drivers try to 'cut' the corner even finer and put the inside front wheel actually off the road. They thus stretch to the limit the radius of the curve described. The advantage of this increase shows up most on very fast bends. In this case the disadvantage of placing a wheel on ground

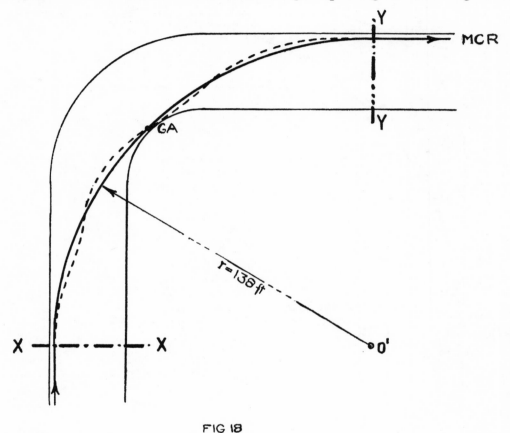

FIG 18

which may have a bad co-efficient of grip is of little account, because the inside front wheel is carrying very little of the car's weight. You have to be careful, though, because there are often stones and other sharp objects just off the roadside which can play havoc with your tyres, damaging the tread or the even more vulnerable sidewall. They may indeed cause injuries to the cords without leaving a visible mark on the rubber, and these lacerations can sooner or later cause a burst—one of the nastiest things that can happen to a driver in racing.

On racing tracks where there is a level infield, they try to prevent this 'grass-cutting' by putting low, sloping kerbs. In road racing, where opportunities of doing it often occur, I always tried to resist the temptation, at least during the first part of the race. In the later stages I sometimes succumbed, but only when it was necessary to gain a few seconds, and never without being conscious of the risk I was running.

THE 'GEOMETRICAL APEX' AND THE 'EFFECTIVE APEX' OR 'CLIPPING POINT' The geometrical apex, GA, is an important point on the corner and you must be able to identify it with precision; from it is derived the 'effective apex' or 'clipping point' which tells you, simply and precisely, the best line to take through a corner. GA can nearly always be found quickly and easily by geometric means, like this: Stroll round the circuit and stand at the point on the corner where the inside edges of the road would intersect if 'produced' (the intersection of the two dotted lines in fig. 19). From this point, which we will call P, look left and right and measure the angle formed by the prolongation of the said edges: 90° in the first case, 135° in the second. A line bisecting this angle crosses the inside of the corner at the point GA, which is what you want.

In some cases you cannot do this because the point P falls outside the roadway, as happens on corners sharper than a right angle. The point GA can here be found by halving the linear distance along the curve xy on the inside of the corner.

If the pieces of straight which precede and follow a corner are not of equal width, the position of the point GA will have to be altered: left later if the exit straight is the narrower, brought nearer if this is the wider of the two (fig. 20B). I indicate this new point by the letter Z, and shall refer to it as the 'effective apex' or 'clipping point'. This is the most important spot on the whole corner, and, as we shall see better later on, altering its position will give all sorts of 'line' through the corner.

It should here be made clear that this point Z, except in the special case shown in fig. 20B, always comes after the point GA. Drivers who 'hug the rails' *before* arriving at GA never manage to achieve a line of constant maximum radius; either they have to slow down, or, worse, if they are already 'on the limit' they may run out of road. (fig. 21).

CONNECTING LINKS In addition to its rotary movement around point O (the centre of the curve being taken), the car is subject also to a turning moment about a vertical axis passing through its centre of gravity, G (fig. 11). In fact, for one complete turn around O, there is a corresponding complete turn about the centre of gravity G. The motion around O, as we have seen, generates centrifugal force; that about G produces no inertia effects until the turning moment attains a constant velocity. At the beginning and at the end of any corner taken at speed, and when the car is sliding, this second motion will vary according to changes in the inclination of the longitudinal axis of the car, AG, with respect to the path being followed (ab in fig. 11), an inclination which, as we shall see, corresponds to its

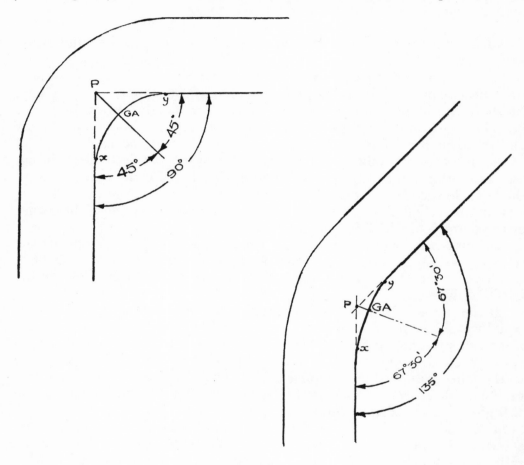

FIG 19

'drift'. From the cockpit you get the impression that the car is rotating about a point A situated between the front wheels, and this impression is supported by the fact that it is these wheels that you are trying to make follow the line that you have chosen; the centre of gravity, meanwhile, is thrown outwards in relation to the front end whenever the car goes into a corner or 'breaks away' at the back, only returning to the original line when the car begins to straighten up on leaving the corner. During these stages, the rotary

48

XIII. *Above:* Nuvolari in an Auto Union at Donington in 1938.

ow: During the G.P. of Monaco in 1936 Achille Varzi (Auto Union) is caught by the camera as he almost literally
clips his 'clipping point' for the corner by the Tobacconist's Corner.

XIV. *Above:* Aintree, 1957. Jean Behra (Maserati) takes a fast corner with his wheel on the white line. The driver of t
car behind is placing himself beautifully for the corner, right on the outside.

Below: The same corner being 'cut' by Peter Collins who has one wheel over the edge. The car behind is about a
yard and a half from the edge of the road, its driver not bothering much about the need for starting a corner from
the outside.

movement about the point O undergoes an acceleration or a deceleration. Inertia effects are set up which tend to oppose or encourage the car's turning moment about its own vertical axis passing through G. These effects vary in inverse ratio to the time spent in carrying out the manœuvre, and so you should reduce them so far as possible by smoothing out your path into and out of the corner; in the first part of your approach, this is to prevent the car going straight on at a tangent because of the forces tending to oppose its turning, and, in the second part of this phase, it ensures that the turning

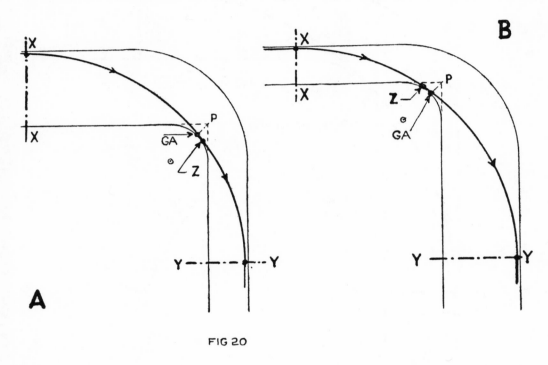

FIG 20

movement, once begun, does not get out of hand, causing the tail to slide too far and eventually put the car into a spin. Similar action is needed on leaving the corner, but you will find this much simpler—almost automatic, in fact, as it is mostly taken care of by the self-centering action of the steering, slowed down a bit if need be by a light grip on the wheel.

To allow for the smoothing-out processes just described, the ideal maximum-constant-radius course has to be modified, as shown in fig. 22, by the addition of two 'connecting curves' of variable radius, the approach having a contracting radius and the exit an expanding one, so as to link the central constant-radius phase 1–2 smoothly with the straight pieces of road before and after the corner.

49

CORNERING IN THREE STAGES By reason of these linking curves, our theoretical 'line of maximum constant radius' in fig. 16 now breaks down into three stages, resulting in a slightly greater distance being covered (see fig. 22), and the points BC and FC, where actual cornering begins and finishes, no longer coincide with the reference lines XX and YY, being

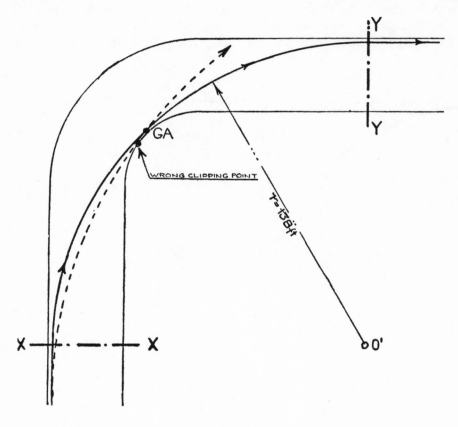

FIG 21

earlier and later respectively. The new central phase 1-2, being shorter, has a smaller radius.

At point 2 begins the linking curve, drawn with an expanding radius, that leads out of the corner. From this point on the speed of the car can be increased by giving more throttle. If this is already wide open, friction between the car and the road will diminish as the radius expands.

It is interesting to observe how, by shortening the time, and therefore the length, of the connecting curves, the amount by which the central constant-radius phase has to be shortened can be reduced to a minimum.

You will see this better on looking at the example in fig. 23, where the lengths of the connecting curves have been purposely exaggerated in relation to the actual type and dimensions of the corner illustrated.

Inside our usual 90 degree corner in a road 33 feet wide, we have seen that it is theoretically possible to inscribe a curve having a constant radius of 138 feet. For a four-wheeled vehicle, as we have already said, this radius

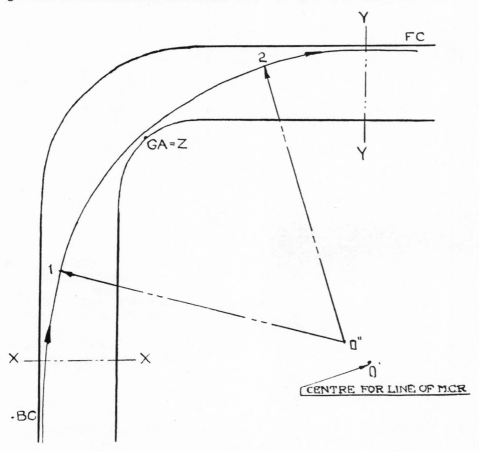

FIG 22

must be reduced, the reduction amounting in the example quoted to three times the width of the car's track. This can be demonstrated geometrically. As the central constant-radius portion has to be sandwiched between two connecting curves B'C–1' and 2'–F'C, each about 40 feet long, this mid section will now have a radius of only 131 feet and the theoretical maximum speed for this second type of 'line' will come down from 41 m.p.h. to 40 m.p.h. Further lengthening of the connecting curves can only shorten the

51

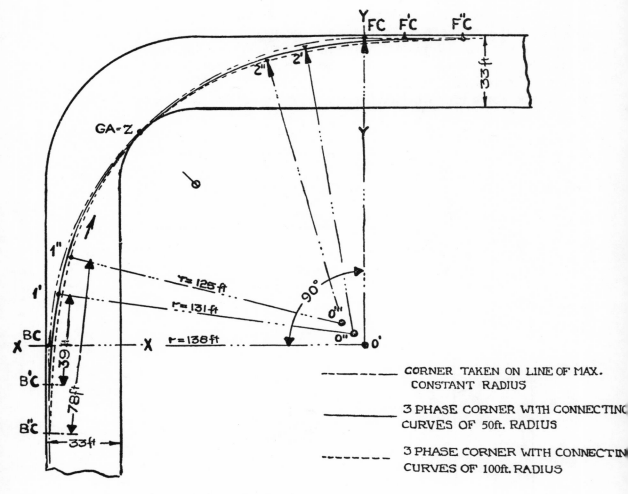

CORNER TAKEN ON LINE OF MAX. CONSTANT RADIUS

3 PHASE CORNER WITH CONNECTING CURVES OF 50ft. RADIUS

3 PHASE CORNER WITH CONNECTING CURVES OF 100ft. RADIUS

FIG 23

radius of the middle section still more, and therefore make the whole corner slower. In this particular case, increasing the connecting curves (B″C–1″ and 2″–F″C) to 78 feet will cause the radius of the mid section to shrink to 125 feet, and bring the speed down to 38·9 m.p.h. Hence the need to take the connecting curves in the shortest possible time.

'Three-phase' cornering, which we have so far only considered in theoretical form, can also be realized in practice—after certain modifications. The first and most important of these is to make sure that you have a certain safety margin for the occasions when, cornering on the limit, you have to cope with the inevitable inequalities of the road surface—and any errors of judgment, however slight. Coming out of the corner at the point

F′C one should not actually touch the roadside but keep a short distance from it. In most cases a yard is plenty. All drivers allow some margin of safety whatever sort of corner they are taking, and only when trying for a lap record, or when tactical considerations require extra high speed, is it relaxed accordingly.

Putting the above consideration into practice, we get a new 'line' through the corner, shown dotted in fig. 24. This, as you will see by comparing it with the 'theoretical' course drawn in fig. 22, lies farther to the outside before the 'clipping point' Z, and closer to the inside thereafter. This 'line' gives a slightly shorter radius, and must therefore be taken at a lower speed, but it does provide the margin of safety that is so necessary everywhere on the corner, and especially on the way out, where mistakes are generally expensive—especially the mistake of going too fast.

The theoretical reduction in speed due to the smaller radius is made up for in practice because, thanks to this margin, you are much less liable to get into slides, which are especially to be avoided during the last part of any corner as they always entail a loss of speed, and this cuts down your speed on the following straight.

To obtain these departures from the theoretical line, the 'clipping point' Z (whose position in fig. 22 coincided with the geometrical apex GA) must be moved farther down the road.

A movement of some 4–6 per cent along the internal arc xy is quite considerable, about 3ft 3ins in the case of our usual illustration, where the arc xy measures 52·5 feet. A consequence of this displacement—or rather the reason for it—is a postponement of the moment when actual 'cornering' begins. The starting point BC, which in the theoretical 'line' (fig. 22) came before the line XX, has moved level with it (point B′C in fig. 24), and in some cases it may be even farther on. In the foregoing I have purposely left the discussion of B′C until after that of point Z (although the former comes first on the road) because it is Z, the 'clipping point' or 'effective apex', that you must mainly concentrate upon as you arrive at a corner and decide on your line. Knowledge of the exact instant for locking over will come with practice, and it will be instinctive once you have settled the 'clipping point' Z, which you have to brush with your front inside wheel while endeavouring to achieve the shortest possible connecting curve. I keep referring to point Z, but this does not mean that you need not pay attention to the position of B′C.

If you want to try out in practice the ideas we have been discussing, and others which are to follow, I advise doing so, to start with, on a flat corner where it is possible to put up clearly visible signs showing the position of the points GA, Z and the line XX. Go through repeatedly, first at reduced speed and then faster and faster, keeping the eye always on point Z. Start turning the steering wheel at an imaginary point BC, situated before the line XX, and try, each time round, to postpone it a little, until it eventually reaches— or even passes—this line. When, starting to 'corner' at XX by turning the wheel quickly and decisively through the proper number of degrees, you succeed in brushing point Z, you will have managed, near enough, to steer the course described in fig. 24. That is the 'drill' on a previously prepared piece of road. In learning a closed circuit, I advise you always to settle at

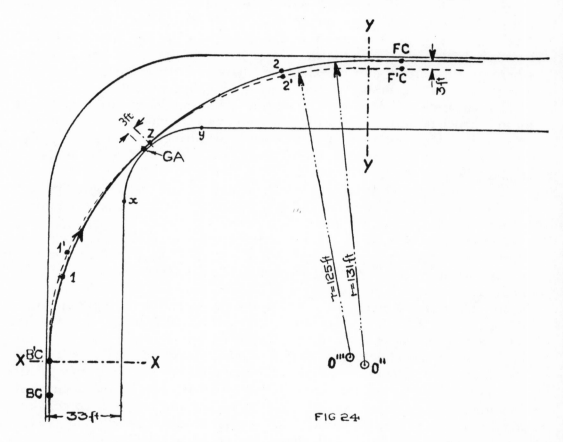

FIG 24.

least where point Z lies, which is relatively easy by our geometrical method. Once you have done so, pick out and memorize a reference mark—a bush, a tree, a post or whatnot, that can be easily identified as you come down into the corner.

In road races like the Mille Miglia, where it is not possible to know the shape of every corner and, hence, its effective apex or 'clipping point' Z, drivers tend to make a rather wide and slow approach-curve, to allow for adjustments while actually cornering that will bring them fairly close to their effective apex Z. But you have no time for these hesitations on a properly learned closed circuit, where every corner should be taken on the limit. For every corner, for every type of machine, the 'effective apex' point Z is clearly defined, and so is the starting point, B′C.

If, through anticipating your B′C point, the car is given too little lock, you will have the trouble shown in fig. 23, or, worse still, find yourself on the line shown in fig. 21; if you steer too quickly, you will have momentarily to take some lock off to get back on the proper line. In either case you will lose speed. If you leave your B′C a bit late, you will be obliged to slide the car too much—which means a loss of time and speed, especially on cars with poor acceleration. If B′C is left *much* too late you will get into a bad slide, or worse still 'run out of road'. The timing of this approach phase is more readily studied in motor-cycle racing, where you can watch the rapidity with which riders lay their machines over.

The possibility of shortening the approach curve will depend not only upon the driver, but also upon the design of the vehicle. Cars that are low-built, light and free from roll, or, to employ more technical terms, which have a low centre of gravity, and a low moment of inertia in the rolling plane, require less time for their approach. It behoves you, therefore, to plan this phase of your 'corner' according to the characteristics of the car you are driving. Skill consists in getting the best possible performance from each.

As you go into a corner, you should turn the steering-wheel not in a series of jerks, but in one smooth, swift movement, checking it as soon as you have enough lock on for the constant radius curve. For a short approach curve of the type shown in fig. 24, the movement takes one-fifth or two-fifths of a second. A slightly longer time is needed on fast bends, and on sharp corners requiring more than half a turn of the steering-wheel.

The constant-radius type of course illustrated up to now can be used when one corner is followed immediately by another, or by a very short piece of straight, and in the sort of corners where the car is not capable of greatly increasing its speed during the exit phase. With this line the corner is taken in the smallest possible time, because it has been driven almost entirely on a radius that is constant and of maximum length. In this case, however, the car's exit speed is theoretically the same as its speed for the entire corner and the driver can increase it only at the very last, when he has already embarked upon the straight.

Pay special attention to the exit phase of a corner. If you get off the 'line' normally used by other competitors, you may find that the road gives a worse grip, because the part the cars do not generally run upon keeps less clean. Examine the surface of the circuit after a race and you will easily see where the cars have been: particularly on the corners and in parts used for braking or acceleration, it shows dark 'tram lines' due partly to rubber left by the tyres. These are the parts where the road 'grips' best—when it is dry. Sometimes, however, it happens that a car will drop oil—in which case the picture changes and things become rather perilous. So watch out for oil! Sometimes it pays to change your 'line' and use a bit of road that is cleaner, even if this means shortening the radius of your curve. Braking and acceleration are then done, sometimes with advantage, on the inside of the straights before and after the corner.

Organizers station flag marshals along the course, whose duty it is to keep in touch with one another, and to advise drivers when there is oil on the track by waving a yellow flag with red vertical stripes. When the damage causing the loss of oil happens unexpectedly, as when an engine 'throws a rod', warning cannot always be given in time. Often the oil patch is difficult to see. The competitor who is unlucky enough to be first on the scene is usually destined to lose control, and often goes off the road. Those behind may get some warning, either from seeing their comrade depart into the scenery, or through the timely action of a marshal who—more by instinct than eyesight—has guessed the state of the road, and waved the appropriate flag. If your machine is losing oil for any reason, signal the fact at once to the marshals, as every second's delay could mean a fatal accident.

By fully exploiting the 'available width of the road', as we have already seen, you can steer a course having a far greater radius than that of the corner itself, and so get round in a much shorter time. If the corner is preceded and followed by straight road, your cornering line will govern the speed attainable on these straights, at any rate when these are at least as long as the course taken through the corner itself. If you can go into a corner a few miles an hour faster, it means that your braking point is postponed—and hence that this phase of the job occupies less time. The same applies to the exit phase, and the time taken for the ensuing straight.

The deceleration brought about by braking, moreover, is far greater than the acceleration that can be imparted to a car by its engine. The acceleration, when the car has only two driving wheels, and only half its weight pressing on these, cannot even in the best conditions, i.e. with extremely powerful engine and a low gear-ratio, exceed 50–60 per cent of the deceleration figure. Cars of poor power/weight ratio can hardly attain 20–30 per cent of it, even in the lower gears, while in top they may get only 10–15 per cent, falling away to zero as maximum speed is approached. It follows that the time taken to slow from a speed of X to a speed of Y m.p.h. is far shorter than the time required to accelerate from a speed of Y to a speed of X. For this reason it is the *exit* phase of a corner that is the most important. The popular dictum that one should 'go in slow, and come out fast' is based partly upon these considerations. Taking the approach at a

XV. *Above:* To prevent drivers from 'grass-cutting' at Monza, the organizers have built sloping kerbs. Farina (20) and Ascari (22) have just taken what used to be called Porphyry Corner.

Below: At Aintree, however, they use a sort of fence. The drivers are Hawthorn and Schell.

XVI. *Above:* Two ways of taking it. As this corner is almost a hairpin, the right course is the one being taken by car number 38 (Taruffi in a Cisitalia). This is also the line followed by the majority of competitors, as witness the black marks on the road. The car numbered 36 is badly placed, and its driver will not be able to go round on the maximum radius.

Below: Mario Tadini, three times winner of the Stelvio hill-climb and recognized 'hairpin' expert. Note the beautiful placing as he comes out of the corner, all ready to accelerate away. His 'clipping point' is almost at the end of the corner.

VII. *Above:* At the Penya Rhin G.P. at Barcelona in 1954 Fangio (Mercedes-Benz) brushes his 'clipping point' on a right-angle corner.

Below: . . . and here, on the same corner, and with the same point, is Mike Hawthorn.

XVIII.

A: Here Fangio (2) and Moss are seen taking a corner in the Penya Rhin G.P. at Barcelona in 1954.

B: The same drivers going into the corner and . . .

C: . . . coming out of it.

lower speed than the run out also gives a greater margin of safety, and makes it easier to choose the right 'line'. If the corner is preceded by a straight, braking is done rather sooner, but time lost by this is less than the amount you gain by being able to accelerate earlier on emerging on to the straight. The loss or gain varies in proportion to the times required in braking and acceleration respectively. From these general considerations let us go on and see how still more time can be saved.

'COMING OUT' EARLY FROM A 'THREE-STAGE' CORNER. If the straight piece after a corner is long in relation to the corner itself and your car has good acceleration, so that you arrive at line YY going several m.p.h. faster than your opponent, you will cash in on this extra speed, or most of it, all down the straight.

To reach YY at a higher speed, you must start accelerating as soon as possible while in the corner. Your line is no longer that of fig. 22, namely maximum constant radius followed by a short exit-line; you must begin your exit phase by the half-way mark and rapidly widen its radius (see fig. 25). As you 'put your foot down', coming out of the corner, the expanding radius permits a gradual increase in speed, and you cross YY faster than in figs. 22 or 24.

The whole 'line' through the corner has therefore been modified: the starting point BC of the approach has been postponed, so that in fig. 25 it comes *after* the line XX. The central constant-radius phase is taken on a shorter radius and therefore at lower speed. The 'clipping point' Z has undergone a second and larger displacement in relation to the geometrical apex GA and has moved farther down the road by an amount which can be as much as 10 per cent or more of the internal arc xy. The acceleration-point 2 comes considerably earlier, and may even come before the 'clipping point' Z. The third phase, 2–F'C, is longer and of very varying radius.

In this case the time occupied in actual 'cornering' may be greater by some tenths of a second, but this is conveniently made up for by the shorter time taken on the ensuing straight. This sort of line is particularly recommended when the car has good acceleration from the speed at which it can take the corner, and when the time discrepancy between its powers of deceleration before the corner and its capacity to accelerate after it is small.

Instantaneous measurements of acceleration are taken with an instrument called an accelerometer.* However, you can easily manage with a stopwatch and the speedometer on the car; you just have to find out what increase in speed the car is capable of developing in a second. The lower the gear in which you make the trial, the greater, naturally, will be the acceleration.

* e.g. Tapley Performance Meter.

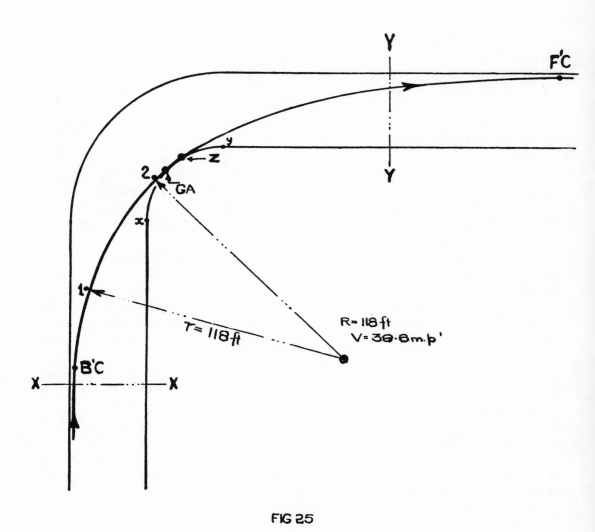

FIG 25

Cars which have a power weight ratio of roughly 100 b.h.p. per ton, fully laden, (those for example which weigh 20 cwt and develop 100 b.h.p.) can, in a low gear such as second, exceed an acceleration of 6 m.p.h./sec. It should be borne in mind that when a car is taking a corner 'on the limit' its capacity for acceleration is reduced, by friction; often too it suffers through loss of traction because the inside rear wheel spins. The driver has to allow for this too. In the example in fig. 25, the stretch we call 1–2 has a constant radius of 118 feet and can be taken at 38·6 m.p.h., i.e. roughly 56 ft/sec. If from 2 the driver can raise this speed by 3 m.p.h./sec. (equivalent to 4·4 ft/sec.), he will arrive at YY (which is 111·5 feet from 2) after 1 4/5

58

seconds doing more than 43·5 m.p.h. Naturally, the 'line' from 2 to F'C must be one which, by its expanding radius, will allow this increase in speed. With our earlier constant-radius method, the YY line was crossed at only 41 m.p.h. That method shows a time for taking the whole corner from XX to YY which is slightly *better* by one-tenth of a second, because the whole 216 feet stretch can be driven at roughly 41 m.p.h., while our newer method gives an average speed of about 40. But with the new method, the car is going some 1·8 m.p.h. faster when it reaches the straight.

This method presents an infinite number of solutions, depending upon the variability of the radius in phase 3, 2–F'C—solutions that depend entirely upon the position chosen for the 'clipping point' Z. The farther this point is pushed beyond the 'geometrical apex' GA, the greater will be the expansion we can give to the radius from 2 to F'C and therefore the greater the acceleration that can be attained. A clever driver will base his tactics upon the accelerating powers of his car. Ten per cent movements for the 'clipping point' Z are fairly normal, and these, as we have seen, are brought about only by corresponding displacements of point B'C.

An especially marked application of the second system will be found suitable for hairpin bends where, owing to the low speed at which they are taken, and to the fact of being in low gear, nearly any car—especially when fitted with a self-locking differential—has enough power at its disposal for rapid acceleration.

As fig. 26 shows, there is a great difference between the course of maximum constant radius (dotted line) and our three-phase treatment using an early exit-curve (solid line): not only because of the difference in radii (from 65 to 50 feet) but also because of the different 'placing'. The first part of the corner is taken wide, and steering is left rather late, so that B'C comes 14 or 15 feet beyond line XX. The 'clipping point' Z is some 13 feet beyond the apex GA, a distance amounting to about 13 per cent of the internal arc xy which is 100 feet long.

If we apply the same calculations to a hairpin as we have done to our right-angled corner, working out the time taken for a maximum-constant-radius treatment and also the speed attained on crossing the exit-line YY, we shall find that the stretch XX–GA has been covered about 2/5 of a second faster under MCR than under the new system, because the average speed on a constant radius is 28 m.p.h. and only 25 on our new course. It is on the latter part of the corner that the new method shows to advantage. In fact, by using the maximum possible acceleration (which for a car driving on the rear wheels only on a non-slip road surface can be as much as 9 m.p.h./ sec.) a car will reach the exit line YY—even though its performance falls far short of this theoretical maximum—at a speed of more than 30 m.p.h. This will enable it to win back, within the first 40 to 50 yards, all the time lost

59

in the first part of the corner, and to go on increasing its advantage all down the straight.

I have noticed that the majority of drivers who are not used to fast and powerful cars take a cornering line in which their 'clipping point' Z almost

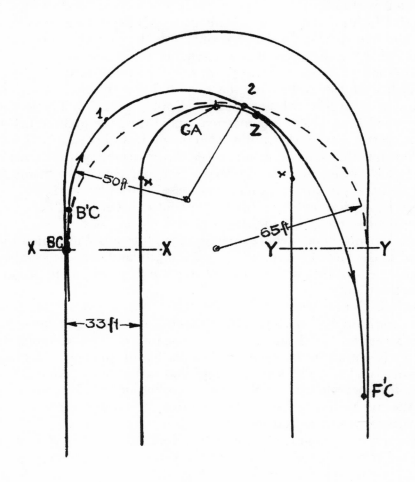

FIG 26

coincides with the geometrical apex GA; they start locking over (BC) too soon and go in slowly. This method is all right on corners which can be taken without lifting the foot—it gives the longest radius (because Z coincides with GA) and it is the fastest; then, too, with the slow approach and early start there is less roll and therefore less friction due to scrubbing of the tyres. Friction is particularly hard on the less powerful cars because while they are actually cornering they cannot regain the speed they have lost. In driving fairly slow cars there is usually a preponderance of 'flat out' corners, as compared with slower ones which require braking and acceleration. This is why drivers of touring cars often take the sort of line I have described, and get into trouble when given a car with better acceleration; they never get outstanding results until they have adjusted their 'line' to suit the requirements of the faster car.

This is why I have made such a point of expressing the movement of Z as a percentage of the roadside arc xy—I want you to realize that this idea is extremely important with any type of car, if you are to make good time on circuits where there are corners followed by straights—which means practically everywhere. In these cases you have to accelerate steadily and continuously—and begin doing so as early as possible. You will be able to do this accurately only if your approach line has been properly laid, and you have found the Z point that gives maximum performance with the acceleration characteristics of your car.

If the corner to be taken is very long, as when the radius is large and the curvature is 90° or more, drivers of cars with good acceleration must postpone their Z point a very long way—sometimes by as much as 15–20 per cent of the distance xy. There is so much road still to come after the mid-point GA that if the throttle were to be opened at that point, the build-up of speed would quickly become excessive. Examples like the Curva Grande on the road circuit at Monza and numbers 5 and 6 at Vallelunga (figs. 35D and 35E) differ from those shown in figs. 25 and 26 only in having a much longer radius. It will be seen that the 'clipping point' Z has been moved a long way beyond GA—in fact by 25 per cent of the arc xy. On the Curva Grande this would mean a distance of about 120 yards.

Sometimes on this sort of corner, which is very long in proportion to the width of the road, it pays to forsake the line of maximum radius and to 'hug the rails' instead, if the inside of the bend offers a better grip or you can take advantage of the camber.

TWO-STAGE CORNERING   In practice, the three phases of a corner often boil down to two (fig. 27): the 'approach' on a decreasing radius (B′C–1), and an expanding 'exit curve' at the end (2–F′C).

As in the previous method, one starts to give full throttle at point 2, which in this case coincides with point 1.

This is what the best drivers generally do. By steering this course it is possible to 'lose' some surplus speed by putting the car into a drift; this works better than the long approach and earlier braking of our former

61

method. This manœuvre is not easy, and it requires very good hands. It is naturally easiest on slow corners.

In these last two cornering techniques, i.e. those illustrated in figs. 25–27, moving the 'clipping point' Z means that the middle phase has to be taken on a shorter radius and therefore at lower speed. So if you have come in a bit too fast you will find it easier to recover.

THREE-STAGE CORNERING WITH AN EARLY APPROACH If lengthening the exit-curve from a corner by starting it early almost always brings better acceleration into the ensuing straight, the same cannot be said for retarding the approach curve. In the latter case, lengthening the approach would mean reducing the radius of the central phase, as shown in figs. 22 and 23. This will not happen if you start your opening gambit so early that you have completed your approach by the line XX, as shown in fig. 28.

To take this particular 'line', you have to bring your B′C a long way inboard—in this case, to a point near the crown of the road. The approach curve, which starts off at an angle to the straightaway, must be preceded by another, very gradual 'anti-curve' A–B′C, leading from the right-hand side to the middle of the road. Anti-curve and approach curve are taken as a very gentle and elongated S; and provided that part of the preceding straight can be used, and provided also sufficient time and space (especially the former) are available for them to be properly carried out, there is little or no shortening of the radius of the central phase, as in fig. 23. The 'clipping point' Z is moved a little farther down the road. The final phase may be taken either on a constant or an expanding radius, whichever seems best. This 'line' does however require a somewhat earlier braking point.

I learned the advantage of this system many years ago on the Spa circuit (fig. 35G), where the Belgian G.P. is held. The third corner after Stavelot is a fast right-hander with a cottage on the inside, preceded by an even faster bend to the left. The straight piece linking these two is so short that if you come out of the first rather wide you enter the second one on the same line as though you had treated the whole thing as an S-bend, as in the solid line in fig. 35G. As you see, this line is very similar to that shown in fig. 28.

You can also, if you like, come out of the left-hander without taking it wide, because the radius of the bend is so large. You are then placed well to the left, ready to take the following right-handed bend and your line through the corners is shorter. Taking this line (shown dotted in fig. 35G) I never succeeded in getting through the left-hander without lifting. Perhaps a better driver could have done so, as there was very little in it; with me every time I got to a certain point my right foot came off the accelerator. In those days my knowledge of cornering was a little uncertain, and there were many

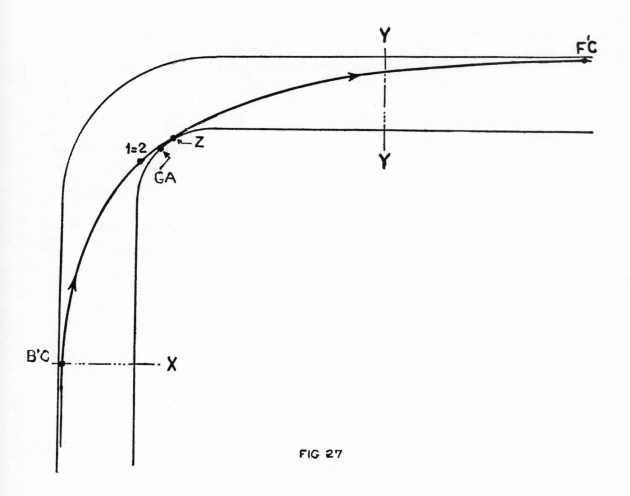

FIG 27

occasions when I was not sure which line to take. I used often to stand at corners and watch, but even those who were reckoned the best drivers did not always use the same method. However, in this particular case they used to come out of the first bend without going wide, and enter the second in the orthodox way.

I have always gone on the principle that a car should make as little friction as possible, and for this reason I always corner on the line of maximum radius, even when this is not necessary. On this occasion I found, acting on this theory of mine, that if I went wide on coming out of the first bend I could get through the next much more easily. After a few laps of practice I finally managed to make it without lifting at all. I have come to the conclusion that the advantage was really due to my starting the approach curve sooner. Often since then I have made a point of using this sort of 'line', although it takes practice because corners vary so much.

I have not seen this method used by other people. It is especially useful on 'open' bends which can be taken nearly flat out. The advantage can be seen by comparing it with the path MCR in fig. 16 and the one in fig. 23, when it will be seen that our new line through the corner is taken on a radius of at least 135 feet.

To my mind this course confers yet another practice advantage. One can

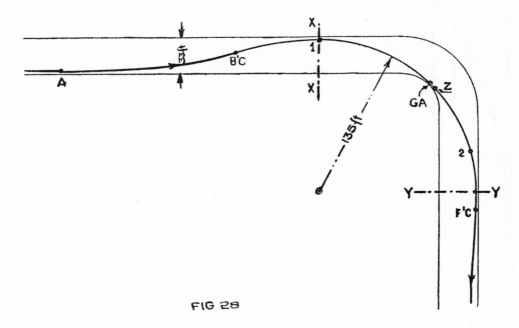

FIG 28

manage to brush the outside edge of the road on a level with XX with much greater ease and precision, while being less likely to get into the trouble shown as C in fig. 17. To drive on the outside of the road for a long way before the line XX when going into a corner is often impossible; the road is often dirtier at the edges, and thus offers a poorer grip. Should it be necessary to put the brakes on, not only will stopping power be diminished, but the car may be thrown off its course. I have found my 'S-line' useful in offsetting these disadvantages and have often used it successfully though in less accentuated form than that shown in fig. 28.

A SUCCESSION OF CORNERS   It is interesting how the 'line' through one corner is influenced by that which succeeds it when the latter is followed by a long piece of straight. Here, too, you should apply the principle of

XIX. *Above:* Jean Behra in a BRM at Tobacconist's Corner at Monte Carlo in 1958 starts his approach-curve. See how he starts his line from the extreme right-hand side.

Below: . . . and the same goes for Tony Brooks (Vanwall) and Hawthorn (Ferrari).

XX.

Top: Here we have Tobacconist's Corner seen from a little farther on. Hawthorn has completed his approach phase . . .

Centre: . . . and so has Tony Brooks (Vanwall)

Bottom: . . . also Brabham in the Cooper.

coming out of the final corner at the highest possible speed. It is worth sacrificing a little speed in the first one, taking it on a smaller radius, if this gives a better course through its successor.

This principle is illustrated in figs. 29, 30 and 31. Points 2 and 2' represent the respective points where the driver can open up.

Fig. 29 shows a pair of hairpins. In this case, a short constant radius is used for the first, so that the second can be taken on a longer radius, which expands on the way out.

Fig. 30 shows a succession of two 90° corners in opposite directions,

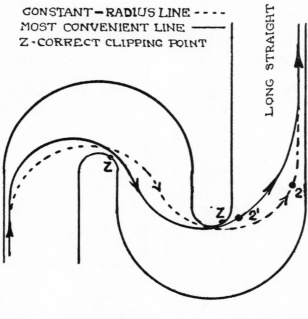

FIG 29

joined by a short straight. It would be possible to treat them as two curves of equal radius (dotted line); it is better however to take the first on a short constant radius, and the second on a wider, expanding one (solid line). In the case of a steeply cambered road, the correct course is approximately that shown in the dotted line.

Fig. 31, on the other hand, shows two 90° corners in the same direction, joined by a straight of such length that it would be possible to take them as a single corner on a constant radius of 115 feet. In this case, by going wider at the start and taking the first half on a constant radius of 98 feet, you could take the second part on an expanding radius. But here, too, if the road is heavily cambered it is better to follow the dotted line.

Fig. 32 shows how to take a 'chicane'. By choosing the course drawn as a solid line, it is possible to make three curves of 147 feet radius; the dotted line gives a radius of only 118 feet, entailing a theoretical drop in speed (assuming an adhesion factor of ·8) from 42·5 to 38 m.p.h.

Figs. 33 and 34 show a corner where the radius of the actual roadway

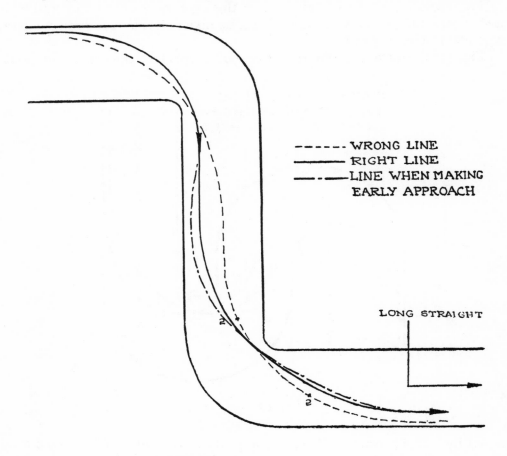

FIG 30

varies considerably. That in fig. 33, in which the road has an expanding radius, is the easier to take, even on first acquaintance. At first sight the road looks narrower than it is, because after the first third the greatly increased radius gives much more room. Not knowing it, one would be inclined to take it at far below its real speed. The reverse holds good when meeting it from the other direction, as in fig. 34. On the road 'blind' corners of this sort are the most dangerous of all, and if you are 'really motoring' you may find it difficult to get round. It is therefore absolutely essential to be warned in advance, and race organizers should put up proper notices. In circuit racing this danger does not arise; the problem of cornering is simply a question of taking the right 'line'.

In figures 33 and 34 I have used dotted lines for the constant-radius curves and solid lines for those with an expanding radius. In these cases, the

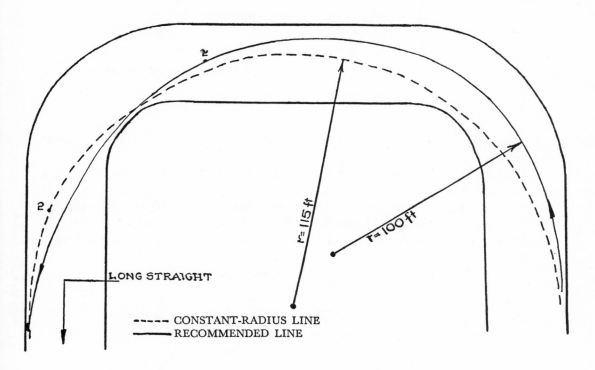

FIG 31

path chosen follows a characteristic, though reversed, pattern. The clipping point in the expanding radius corner comes before the halfway mark; on the corner that 'tightens up' it is more than two thirds of the way round.

If these corners follow one another, it is not a good idea to take the shortest path, because you lose the benefit of the larger radius. There are a few rare exceptions to this, due to peculiarities of the road itself and exigencies of overtaking. Another is when you arrive at the first of a series of corners under the brakes. In this case, to put off your braking point it may pay to sacrifice some speed on corner II and go into it nearer the inside. If II is taken on an even shorter radius, your car is placed better for taking III; this

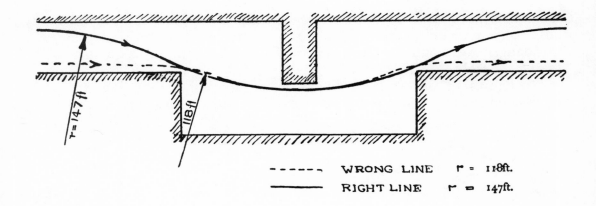

FIG 32

is a good plan if corner III is the last in the series, and is followed by a piece of straight.

An example of this is to be found at Modena, in the series marked 1, 2, 3 on the circuit plan (page 119). As the detailed diagram fig. 35 shows, it is better to take the (solid) line A, than the dotted one B. In the former, the braking point is delayed (from B to B′ in the diagram) and Corner I is taken on a slightly shorter line, and faster. Taking Corner II on a suitably

CORNER WITH INCREASING RADIUS

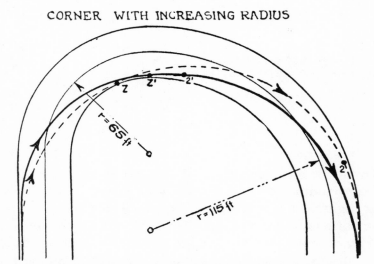

LINE OF EXPANDING RADIUS DURING EXIT PHASE: CLIPPING - POINT AT Z′ ———————

LINE OF CONSTANT MAXIMUM RADIUS: CLIPPING POINT AT Z ———————————

FIG 33

short radius, you are nicely placed for Corner III and can come out of it at the highest possible speed.

Another example is a series of corners on the Imola circuit marked 13, 14, 15 on page 119.

As the diagram in fig. 35A, shows, it is better to take the solid line A. By doing so it is possible to postpone the moment of braking which, on fast cars, should be started in corner number 13. The brakes act more effectively, too,

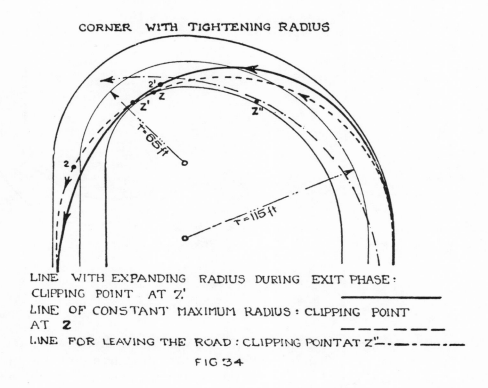

CORNER WITH TIGHTENING RADIUS

LINE WITH EXPANDING RADIUS DURING EXIT PHASE:
CLIPPING POINT AT Z'

LINE OF CONSTANT MAXIMUM RADIUS: CLIPPING POINT
AT **Z**

LINE FOR LEAVING THE ROAD: CLIPPING POINT AT Z"

FIG 34

because this course, A, gives a longer radius for taking corner 13. I have found in this particular case that if you start corner 14 at a point near the inside of the road, its 'line' blends well with that for number 15, and the two can be treated as a single long bend. This is always a good thing, because it eliminates a separate approach curve for the following corner, in this instance number 15.

There is an almost parallel case at Zandvoort (fig. 35B).

Not long after the Pits there is a right-hand loop (1) followed by a series of three corners: a fast pair of left- and right-hand bends (2, 3) leading to a left-hand loop (4). If you wish to take the 'correct' line through

69

4, you will come out of 3 well to the right-hand side of the road (dotted line); but as the straightaway between 3 and 4 is so short, you will have to reduce speed slightly through 3, and treat the straightaway as a right-and-left S-bend. This being so, it is better to forsake the dotted line and follow the one shown solid on the diagram, which gives a higher speed through 2 and 3 and especially on the brief straight 3–4. It also permits braking and acceleration to be effected on the straightaway, so that this stretch is covered in better time. The fact that 4 must now be taken on a somewhat

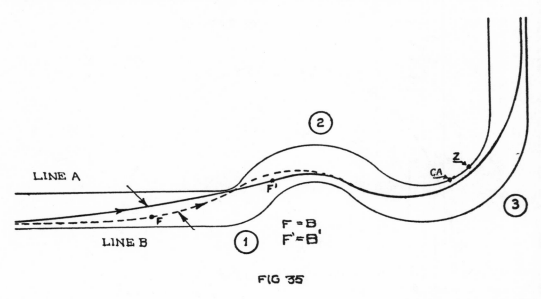

FIG 35

shorter radius is of little importance on such a wide loop. On corners 7 and 8 at Sebring, on the other hand, a different treatment is necessary (fig .35c). Here the proper course is shown by the solid line in the diagram: a right- and left-hand S, because starting the second right-angle nearer the inside (shown dotted at 8 in fig. 35c) means much less shortening of radius here than in the case of the loop at Zandvoort.

'LINES' WHEN OVERTAKING   In racing the rules for overtaking are not those of the Highway Code, but those of the International Competition Regulations (Code Sportif). During a race, moreover, there are flag marshals to warn a competitor when there is someone on his tail by holding out a blue flag and to wave this flag should the man behind be disposed to overtake. In each case the driver in front should give way, keeping well to the right, and assist the overtaker by slowing down if conditions require it, and waving

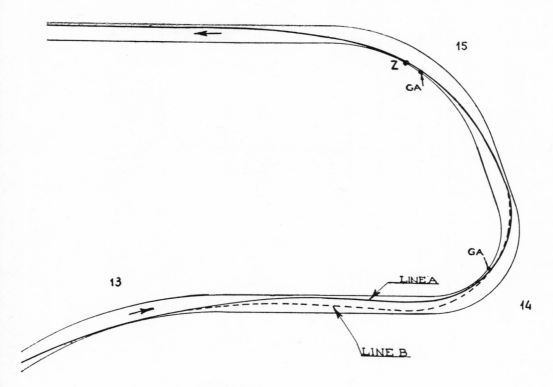

LINE A

LINE B

FIG 35ᴀ

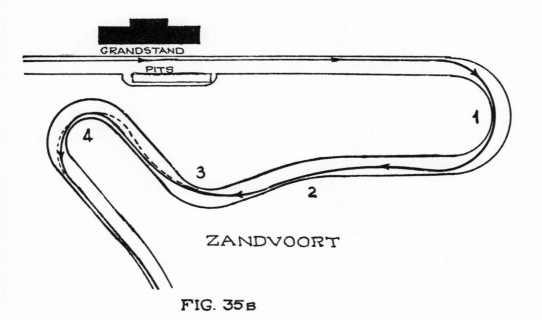

GRANDSTAND

PITS

ZANDVOORT

FIG. 35ʙ

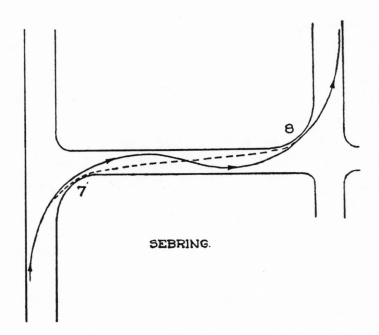

SEBRING.

FIG. 35c

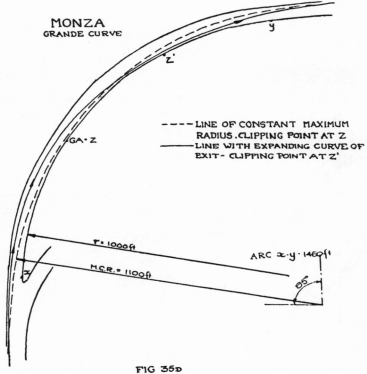

MONZA
GRANDE CURVE

- - - - LINE OF CONSTANT MAXIMUM
RADIUS. CLIPPING POINT AT Z
——— LINE WITH EXPANDING CURVE OF
EXIT- CLIPPING POINT AT Z'

r = 1000 ft

ARC x·y = 1460 ft

M.C.R. = 1100 ft

FIG 35D

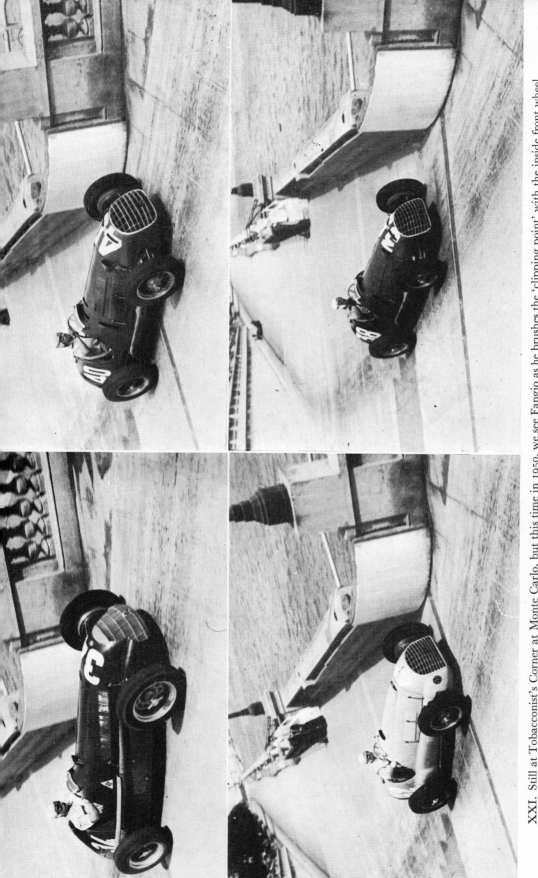

XXI. Still at Tobacconist's Corner at Monte Carlo, but this time in 1950, we see Fangio as he brushes the 'clipping point' with the inside front wheel of his Alfa Romeo 158, and begins the second phase of the corner, on an expanding radius. The angle of the unsteered back wheels and the position of the driver's hand would suggest that the maestro is already accelerating hard, and the car is in a state of oversteer. Some more shots of the same race and same corner showing Ascari (Ferrari) a yard farther back . . . Raymond Sommer . . . and Villoresi.

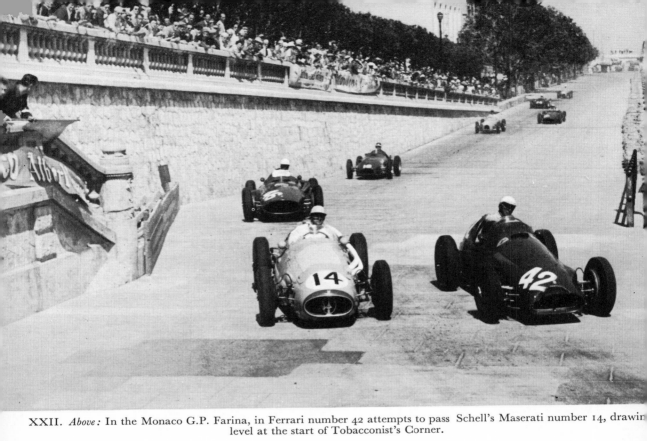

XXII. *Above:* In the Monaco G.P. Farina, in Ferrari number 42 attempts to pass Schell's Maserati number 14, drawing level at the start of Tobacconist's Corner.

Below: Corners in series; a right-hand followed by a left-hander. Coming out of the first, drivers try and keep to the left, so as to be well placed for the second: Peter Whitehead and Sommer at San Remo in 1949, both on Ferrari.

XIII. German Grand Prix, 1951: the same corner being taken by: *Top Left*: Gonzales, (Ferrari); *Top Right*: Ascari (Ferrari)
Centre Left: Villoresi (Ferrari); *Centre Right*: Taruffi (Ferrari); *Bottom Left*: Fangio (Alfa Romeo); *Bottom Right*:
Farina (Alfa Romeo).

XXIV. *Left*: Two left-handers in succession. Drivers endeavour to make two curves into a single long bend of maximum radius. Here we see Fangio (number 18) during his first outing in the supercharged 1½-litre Alfa Romeo 158, followed by Alberto Ascari of the Ferrari team at San Remo in 1950.

Right: Turin, March 27, 1955. The winner, Alberto Ascari takes an S-bend during the G.P. in the Valentino Park.

him on. If the man in front has already embarked on a corner, he has the right to go into it from the outside and come out on the inside; the man wishing to overtake must do so on the outside. National and International regulations sometimes give a conflicting ruling in such matters; in general it is left to the sportsmanship of the driver, who will do all he can to get out of the way, especially if he has already been lapped. To overtake on the outside of a corner as the Code lays down, after what we have established about the theory of cornering, is obviously not possible unless the man in front is travelling at well below the maximum speed, and so badly placed, both going into and coming out from the corner, that there is room between his car and the side of the road for another vehicle to pass.

For this reason drivers have come to an arrangement amongst themselves, and this is now virtually accepted; the man in front goes wide letting the faster car through on the best line with a minimum loss of time. To let the overtaker know whether he is to come past on the right or the left, the man in front waves him on, using the appropriate arm.

Of course when two or more competitors are having a tear-up on equal terms, this no longer holds good. If the man behind can manage to come out of the corner faster, he will carry this advantage with him into the straight. To do this he must study the corner on which his opponent is weakest, and, keeping just the right distance behind as they go into the corner, try and be right on his tail as they come out, and with the greatest possible momentum. On fast corners he will also gain advantage from the slipstream and be sucked along. If only he can manage to draw level, he will be nicely placed, if the first corner is a left-hander, for taking the inside line. The line of entry will not be the ideal one for him, but if he seems really determined his opponent will feel compelled to slow down and let him through, because the very presence of a car there will spoil the line that he was about to take.

With this method it is easy to overtake while braking for a hairpin bend, by virtue of the fact, already discussed, that for a given time interval the distance between two cars varies according to the speed. Close behind his opponent as they arrive at the corner, the driver of car R in figs. 35F(A) and 35F(B) can easily draw alongside and even pass him during the braking period, assuming that V has not braked to the limit and that he has kept to the other side of the road for his approach. Driver R must be careful, however, that the road on which his own braking will have to be done is not unduly slippery. The moment the two cars draw level V is compelled, as we have seen, to give precedence to R. The latter must take the corner more slowly, because his is the smaller radius and V will probably manage to repass as they come out of the corner, having been better placed for the approach, provided that R is not in his way as they emerge. To do this he must have worked out speeds and distances very carefully during the run-in, and must not lock over until very late (BC in fig. 35F(B) so as to come out on an expanding radius and, accelerating before the 'clipping-point' Z, manage not to find R in his way. It becomes a battle of wits, and the craftier type comes off best.

In fig. 35F the two cars, V and R are pictured covering the stretch L–M with a constant time-interval between them, in this case one-fifth of a second. This time interval corresponds to a distance of 33 feet when the cars are travelling at 112 m.p.h., as they will be as they pass line LL (which equals 164 ft/sec.). The distance shrinks to 6.5 feet when the speed of the vehicles drops to 22 m.p.h.

Over the stretch from MM to GA, car R, having a shorter distance to cover (by 3 to 6 ft.) and the advantage of 'pole position', succeeds in drawing level with V.

In fig. 35F(B) car V, having taken a line which allows him to go very wide on his way out, is in a position to re-pass R.

If V does not wish to pass R during the braking period, he should take the line shown dotted in 35F(B) In this case R should attempt the solid line.

These excursions, although helpful in allowing you to overtake, inevitably mean that you will take longer to cover a lap. And this disadvantage often applies to your opponent as well. Keep this well in mind. If the manœuvre has to be repeated often, other competitors in front of you and behind will gain an advantage.

When you are driving as a member of a team, duelling with team mates is to be avoided; it can only benefit the opposition.

2 · *At the Limit of Adhesion*

I have tried to describe the methods of cornering used in racing, and the reasons for taking one 'line' rather than another. Let us now see how to take them on the limit of adhesion, and what you actually have to do.

This is not so easy to demonstrate as the various 'lines'. The instinct for 'limit' cornering depends mainly upon a driver's ability to sense when his machine is about to 'break away' under the influence of centrifugal force, and upon the rapidity of his reflexes in checking its wayward motions by means of the steering-wheel and accelerator.

Owing to the 'drift' brought about by centrifugal force when cornering fast, the car is apt to depart from the line that it would follow if taking the same corner at a moderate speed. The driver has to hold the car to its course by foreseeing and allowing for this drift, which varies according to the design of the car, its speed, and the nature of the road surface.

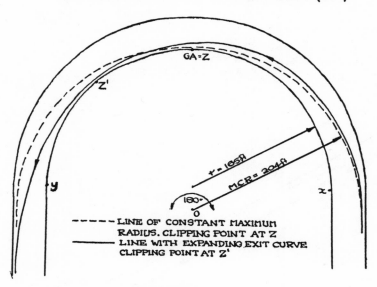

LINE OF CONSTANT MAXIMUM
RADIUS. CLIPPING POINT AT Z
LINE WITH EXPANDING EXIT CURVE
CLIPPING POINT AT Z'

FIG 35 E

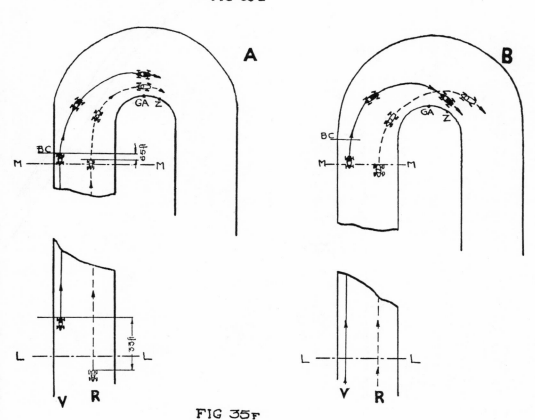

FIG 35F

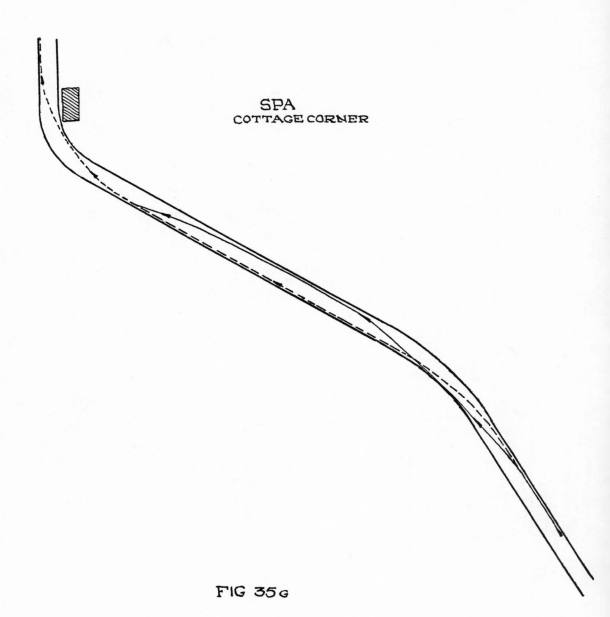

SPA
COTTAGE CORNER

FIG 35 G

If I were asked to describe in a few words *how* to take a corner on the limit, I would say 'go in with the throttle open just enough to hold the car at a steady speed while it goes round, and then open up fully as you come out, provided the engine has enough power'. I should also advise you to make the first trials in a place with lots of room, nothing to get in the way, and a surface offering uniform grip. Aerodrome runways are ideal; I always use them when possible when trying out a strange car, especially for the first few miles. By deliberately taking it beyond the limits of control you can learn its peculiarities much more quickly and safely. And you can mark out examples of every type of corner encountered on the road, and label them at the principal points that we have been discussing: XX, BC, GA, Z, FC and YY. Once the course is marked out you can practise the various kinds of 'corner', first at reduced speed, and then progressively faster until the limit is reached. As you rehearse each type of corner, time after time, you will begin to know, almost instinctively as you lock over at a given speed, how much the car will drift. Then you will arrive, still drifting, and still under perfect control, at your 'clipping point' and start accelerating again.

When you have mastered these techniques on an aerodrome, you can try driving on 'real life' road circuits; but stick to the airfields at first; it is safer—and cheaper—when you run out of road!

THE ATTITUDE OF THE CAR WHILE CORNERING Before starting to motor 'on the limit', it is well to know the technical reasons for the car's behaviour while cornering: once you understand what is happening it is easier to know what to do.

If we compare a car that is taking a corner slowly (fig. 36A) with one that is travelling fast (fig. 36B), you will see that the latter assumes a particular attitude in relation to the direction of travel, giving the impression that it is headed for the inside of the corner. The car is in fact 'drifting' with all four wheels along the predetermined course, its longitudinal axis (and therefore the rear wheels) having assumed a certain angle α tangential to the path that the latter are describing.

For the steered front wheels any such angle is increased by the geometrical angle β (i.e. the amount of lock) required to take the given corner at speed. This angle, in its turn, is modified to a greater or less extent by a second factor ϵ when the corner is taken at high speed.

At speeds approaching zero m.p.h. the tracks of the rear wheels follow a path drawn on a slightly shorter radius than that of the front wheels. When, however, the car is cornered fast, the rear wheels move outwards and follow a curve of wider radius.

If a pneumatic tyre carrying a weight, which in our case is a percentage of the weight of the vehicle, is subjected to a force acting in the plane of the wheel the latter follows a straight-line path. When, however, a force is applied to the tyre at right angles to the wheel plane, as, for example, when encountering a side-wind on a straight road, or when the vehicle is affected by centrifugal force while cornering, it no longer moves in the direction of the wheel plane but at an angle to this, which we call the 'slip angle'. By reason of this attitude, caused by the distortion of the tyre tread and carcase, a reaction is exerted upon the wheels by the road, tending to restore equilibrium. This force is generated more by distortion of the tyre where it makes contact with the ground than by actual slippage and in the language of the British tyre technician, it is called the sideway force or self aligning torque.

As can be seen from fig. 37,A which represents a non-driving wheel of a car viewed from above, the sideway force, acting at right angles to the wheel is composed of two forces (see fig. 37B): a force L, acting at right-

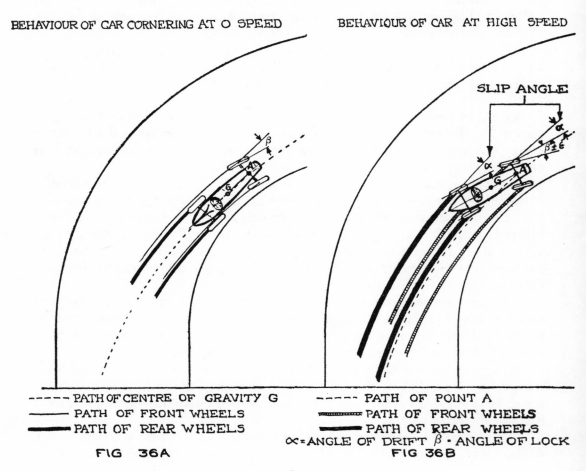

BEHAVIOUR OF CAR CORNERING AT O SPEED   BEHAVIOUR OF CAR AT HIGH SPEED

SLIP ANGLE

- - - - PATH OF CENTRE OF GRAVITY G   - - - - - PATH OF POINT A
———— PATH OF FRONT WHEELS   ············· PATH OF FRONT WHEELS
———— PATH OF REAR WHEELS   ———— PATH OF REAR WHEELS

∝=ANGLE OF DRIFT β · ANGLE OF LOCK

FIG 36A   FIG 36B

78

angles to the direction of travel, which is balanced, during cornering, by centrifugal force; and Drag, R, the sum of all the forces that oppose the forward motion of the car. The former is referred to in modern British technical writings as Cornering Force, but I prefer to think of it as 'Lift', L, because the whole phenomenon is very similar to the behaviour of an aeroplane wing, for which there is an 'optimum' angle of incidence that offers the minimum drag while providing the maximum carrying power or 'lift' from the wing.

The sideway force which the tyres receive from the road rises rapidly—and only at first proportionately—with the angle of drift, up to a maximum

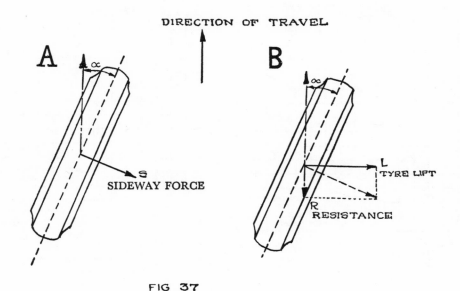

DIRECTION OF TRAVEL

A

SIDEWAY FORCE

B

L TYRE LIFT

R RESISTANCE

FIG 37

value for this angle of 15°–20°, and it varies according to weight-distribution, type of tyre, rim-size, inflation pressure, co-efficient of adhesion and the design of the car. Beyond this angle, slip becomes more important than tyre distortion and sideway force ceases to increase. Side thrust effects can be observed by playing about with tyre pressures and weight distribution between front and rear wheels. By increasing the tyre pressures or the rim width, for example, the slip angle is reduced.

As it is up to the manufacturer, and the driver, to derive the maximum advantage from sideway force these considerations may be helpful during the preparation of an individual car, bearing in mind that handling is simplified when the front tyres provide a larger slip angle than those at the rear.

The two graphs (fig. 38A and 38B) illustrate how slip angles are affected by variations in the co-efficient of adhesion and by the rigidity of the tyres.

The next two graphs, however, show sideway force as a function of two other variables: the load carried by the tyre and the inflation pressure. Note how, for extremely low specific loadings, as found on racing cars shod with very large tyres (see first part of the graph in fig. 39A), side thrust increases in proportion to load.

It must also be borne in mind that although higher pressures should, for

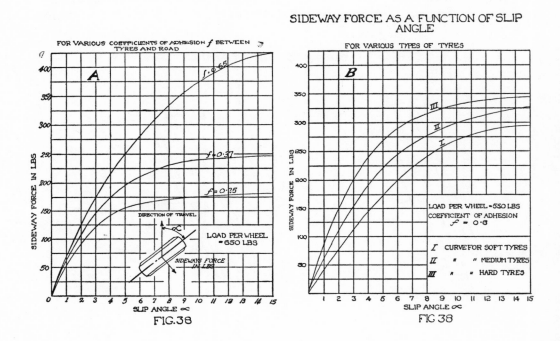

FIG. 38

FIG. 38

a given slip-angle, increase the sideways thrust, the latter may in fact diminish, because very hard tyres grip less well on a loose surface.

FORCES ACTING UPON A CAR WHILE CORNERING   There are three distinct kinds of forces acting upon a vehicle in motion: wind resistance; frictional loads between tyre and road; and finally the various forces and moments of inertia. These forces are always in equilibrium, even though the car is not going in what we may regard as the 'right' direction.

However, as I wish to analyse only the car's behaviour while cornering, for simplicity's sake we will consider only those forces of most interest from the driving point of view: Centrifugal force, Fc, Sideway force S, and Driving force M.

V. *Above:* Fangio opens up while actually in the corner; engine torque brings the tail round into a slightly oversteering attitude.

Below: Schell and Menditeguy in a very fast downhill corner on the Rouen circuit. Both cars are taking this right-hand corner on left-hand lock, showing that they tend to oversteer, especially when, as now, corners are taken on full throttle.

XXVI. *Above:* During the 1957 G.P. at Monza, Fangio is seen overtaking a slower competitor (Brooks in a Vanwall) on the entry to a corner. He has come in at considerably higher speed than his opponent, and is already in process of slowing down, with a very pronounced angle of drift. The front wheels are pointing slightly to the *left*, showing that the World Champion intends to open up already and start coming out of the corner on an expanding radius.

Below: A few yards farther on Fangio has almost drawn level. His angle of drift is smaller: he is starting to accelerate.

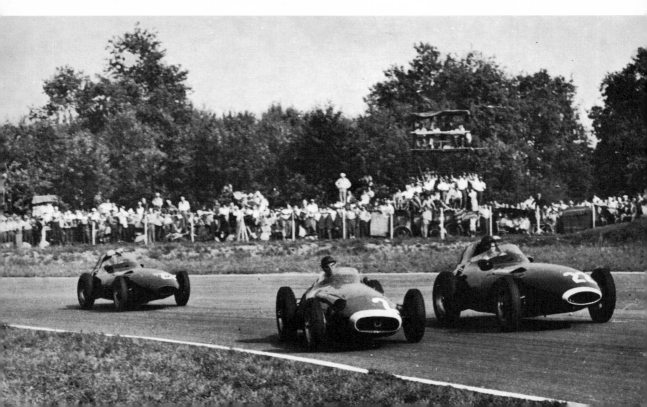

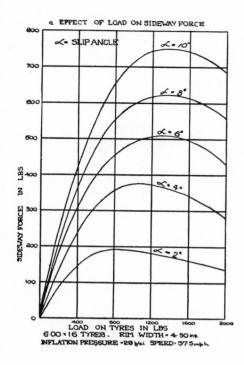

a EFFECT OF LOAD ON SIDEWAY FORCE

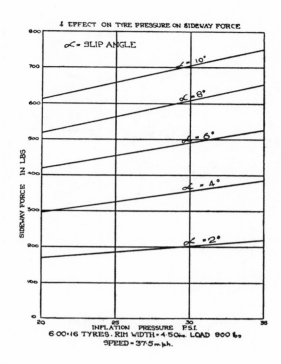

b EFFECT ON TYRE PRESSURE ON SIDEWAY FORCE

FIG 39

The first, which stems from the fact that the car is turning a corner, is concentrated at the centre of gravity of the car, and therefore at some distance above the ground; the other two, which together balance the first, act at ground level, grappling the road, as it were, via the wheels, with a frictional force. The latter, however, cannot ever be greater than Wf, the adhesion factor between tyres and road. Fig. 40A shows, in exaggerated form, the path taken by the car.

Were the car not sliding, it would run off the road on the inside. If, on the other hand, it were suddenly to lose its grip on the road, it would fly off at a tangent in the direction b. However, being subject to all the various forces acting upon it, it describes a curve with centre O′ (path c), sliding slightly with all four wheels.

Fig. 40B shows the same car with all the forces acting upon its wheels marked in. The centrifugal force concentrated at the centre of gravity has been broken down into its various components, which are shown as they affect the wheels.

It will be seen that centrifugal force tends to make the car go off the road while both M and S are trying to keep it there. These two latter forces

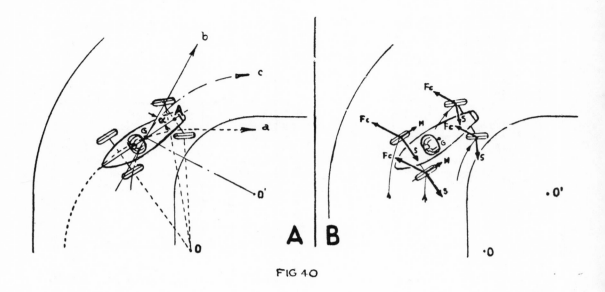

FIG 40

combined accomplish all their 'grappling' at the point where the periphery of the tyre meets the road. So it is understandable why tyres must not be allowed to lose their adhesion.

By turning the steering as he goes into a corner, the driver causes the front wheels immediately to adopt a predetermined angle of lock, β plus the slip angle necessary to receive from the road surface the amount of sideway force required to balance that proportion of the centrifugal component that is acting upon the front part of the car—a force generated as soon as the car enters upon a curved path.

The non-steering rear wheels, however, assume the required angle only by skidding, that is by rotating the whole vehicle about a vertical axis passing through G (see fig. 36). The car's mass, by reason of its inertia, is at first unwilling to do this, but the turning moment, once started, has a tendency to continue. This tendency must be kept in check by the driver.

From this sequence of actions and reactions you can get some idea of the delicacy necessary in handling the steering-wheel, and of how the exit from the corner may depend upon the driver's finesse and his skill in timing the precise movements necessary to hold the car in a drift and thus derive most benefit from 'sideway force', or rather the 'cornering power' of his tyres.

By opening or closing the throttle, moreover, the driver can raise or lower the degree of driving force M, and this too, acting in conjunction with the sideway force S, can balance a large centrifugal force if laid on in the proper doses. In practice this all happens instinctively and not by deliberate planning on the driver's part.

82

We now see diagrammatically (fig. 41) what a judicious combination of M and S can do. In fig. 41A, as before, the wheel is subject to driving force M and sideway force S (solid arrows) which, in combination, give the resultant X (dotted arrow). This acts, as the diagram shows, in the opposite direction to Fc.

Referring now to fig. 41B we find that force X (this time shown as a black arrow) can be broken down into two forces, L and A (dotted arrows). L is the cornering force 'lift' which we met with in fig. 37 as a component of the force S, as applied to the non-driving wheels. A is the force acting in the direction of travel which, having overcome the various resistances to the car's forward motion, will, if still sufficiently large, be available for acceleration.

The frictional force which develops between the tyres and the road (due to S alone, to M alone, or, as in this case, by joint action of the two) cannot ever be greater than the co-efficient of adhesion between tyres and road. Translating this into geometrical terms, therefore, we can say that forces applied to the wheels at ground level cannot have a geometrical resultant X greater than the maximum adhesion factor Lf.

Looking again at the diagrams, we can see, too, how the motive force M, if properly applied, can be used to advantage while cornering. Let us consider, for the sake of example, one of the driving wheels of a car, carrying a load of 550 lb. and travelling in a given direction with a constant slip angle a beyond which, in practice, no increase can be expected from sideway force S. As can be seen from fig. 38 this angle will be somewhere about 10°–15°. If the adhesion factor f between tyres and road is ·8, the force of adhesion Lf is 550 × ·8 = 440 lb.

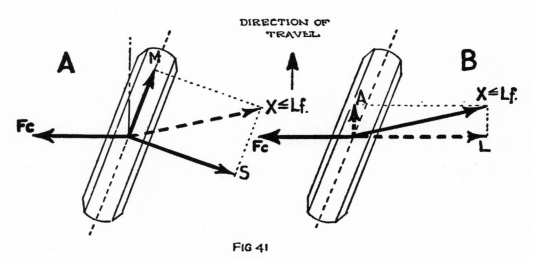

FIG 41

For relatively modest values the driving force M, acting in conjunction with S, has as resultant a force X acting in the opposite direction to that of Fc. In this case L will attain a maximum value, i.e. that of X itself, which can only be, at most, equal to Lf (see fig. 42).

This is a good condition to maintain during the central phase of slow corners. If, however, the driving force M is zero (as when you are running light) or, worse still, negative, as when you lift your foot, the value of L will fall (fig. 43). For greater clarity the diagram below is duplicated to show the two systems of forces. In the first drawing (A) the force X is shown as a resultant of two forces: minus M and S. In (B) this same force X is shown to be made up of two components also: minus A and L. The latter, as the diagram shows, is a smaller quantity than the corresponding L and the one shown in fig. 42. This is what happens when, partly owing to the decrease in the weight pressing the rear wheels down, the car goes into a spin.

If M is very strong, however (see fig. 44a), L is no longer able to assume its maximum value (see fig. 44b) as it did in the case of fig. 42. This occurs when a large amount of torque is applied to the driving wheels, either for rapid acceleration or to overcome the resistances encountered by the car at high speed (see fig. 44c). In the last-named diagram the total drag of the car is assumed to be equal to the force available for advancement, A. In such

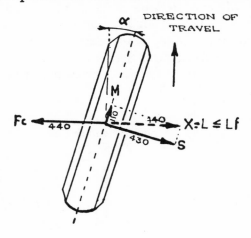

FIG 42

conditions although considerable power is being applied to the driving wheels, the car can only run at a constant speed as in fig. 42—and it enjoys a smaller 'lift' L. To make up for it, the application of torque causes a transfer of weight on to the rear wheels.

Owing to this lessening of cornering force L, the theoretical maximum speed on the graph in fig. 12 is slightly lower on fast corners.

Summing up, the driver must try to bring about the conditions shown in fig. 42 and, when need be, the intermediate states shown in figs. 42 and 44. He must never get himself into the situation we have drawn as fig. 43.

In other words, you must never lift your foot in a corner, but must keep just enough throttle on during the central phase to hold your speed constant,

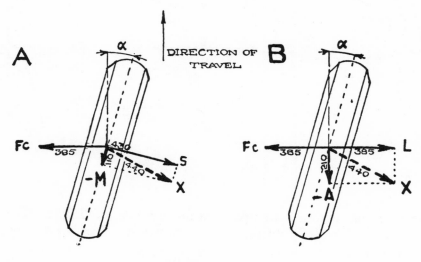

FIG 43

so as to be ready to open up as you leave the corner, widening the radius as you go. The rear driving wheels, particularly during this phase, should be at the limit of adhesion, obtaining the maximum effect from the forces S and M. In this case, the front wheels, having no torque to transmit, assume a smaller slip angle (for a given amount of S) than the driving wheels; therefore, as more and more torque is fed into the latter the angle of lock required to make the front wheels follow a given path must be reduced by a certain factor ε, as described at the beginning of this chapter (see fig. 36B). You find this in racing cars under rapid acceleration and in fast corners where, to overcome the high resistances involved, much torque has to be applied to the driving wheels.

In front-wheel-drive cars, where the front wheels are driven as well as steered, these possess a larger directional capacity only so long as the torque being transmitted does not unduly reduce the 'lift' or cornering force that they can get from the road. This is why front-wheel drive is not suitable for powerful racing cars.

Should the slip angle be allowed to become excessive while cornering, either on purpose or as the result of an involuntary skid, there will be a large

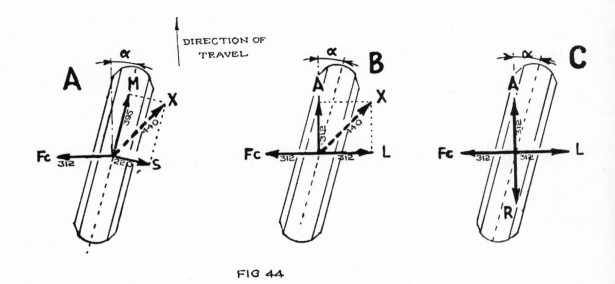

FIG 44

increase in drag, without an appreciable increase of 'lift' L. The latter, moreover, will eventually decline, if the manœuvre has been exaggerated, because the strong scrubbing action of the tyres on the road reduces the value of the co-efficient f; this means a lowering of Lf and, with it, of the value that can be attained by their resultant X.

Very large slip angles should be reserved for occasions when, either deliberately or by mistake, one goes into a corner at a speed over the limit. Having got halfway round, however, i.e. to the point where you want to begin increasing speed, the slip angle must be brought back to regions where it offers the least drag while providing the maximum amount of lift. This is particularly true of low-powered cars.

To drive with small slip angles, on the other hand, means not using all the 'cornering power' of your tyres. Cars seen in this attitude are not being driven really fast.

I have been trying to make you understand the importance of avoiding excessive slip angles, and hence undue sliding about during the second phase of a corner, because this, even if controlled, can only cause unnecessary drag.

A large slip angle is sometimes used by front rank drivers to bring their speed down when entering a corner. This somewhat acrobatic manœuvre is one of the most difficult to carry out; it requires supreme control of the machine and mastery of technique. It is much easier when the corner is slightly banked, as the banking helps to check the rotary moment due to inertia and the excessive slip angle involved.

The course through this type of corner is similar to that described in fig. 27 in the preceding chapter. To take it while slowing down you have to bring your locking-over point BC farther back, so as to give the car a considerable angle of drift—which in some cases may exceed 30°. The movement must be rapid at first and then checked to reduce the inertia moment. Halfway through your 'approach curve' coming into the corner, start accelerating—not hard, but enough to produce greater 'lift'. At 2 before 'clipping point' Z, turn the wheel the other way to increase the radius. The drift angle declines and you are then in a position to open up fully, taking the expanding exit-link under full acceleration. The amount of accelerator in this manœuvre is very critical, since the car is being controlled mainly on the throttle. Considerable torque is required, and so the technique is easier to accomplish on cars with plenty of power.

UNDERSTEERING AND OVERSTEERING CARS   Owing to torque effects, and the way the amount of sideway force varies due to the numerous factors we have been discussing, it is unlikely that the slip angles for the front wheels will ever be the same as those of the back wheels. The driver, therefore, does not just have to turn the steering-wheel through the number of degrees needed to steer the 'geometrical' course; he must be continually turning it one way or the other, so that, with the relative slip angles of front and rear wheels constantly changing, he can achieve a state of equilibrium at the road wheels between the lateral forces and those tending to balance them out.

The proportion of slip as between the front wheels and the rear ones determines the oversteering or understeering behaviour of the car. This will also depend upon the chassis design.

A car is said to understeer when, in taking a corner of given radius at a high and constant speed, the steering has to be turned through a greater angle, $\beta + \epsilon$, as compared with the angle, β, required when taking the same corner at a speed close to zero m.p.h. It is said to oversteer when it requires a smaller angle (see fig. 36B). In the former case, the car shows greater unwillingness to take the corner and, if the driver wishes to take the same curve at higher speed, he must turn the steering through a greater number of degrees. Conversely, in the case of oversteer, for a given amount of lock the car tends to accentuate the corner, and head for the inside verge.

GOING INTO THE CORNER   I do not advise changing gear as you start going into a corner, as some drivers do, because the act of changing often causes changes in rear wheel adhesion, if only to a limited extent. And, however short the time taken by this operation, it is better to devote both hands to the task of steering, especially on fast corners. A possible exception

87

is the slow corner illustrated in the chapter on braking; here your changing can be done during the entry phase—but not thereafter.

All braking should have been done on the straightaway before the corner, and you should go into your approach curve without touching the brakes again, and with your foot poised upon the accelerator, ready to open up at the proper moment.

During the first part of the approach curve, as I have already indicated,

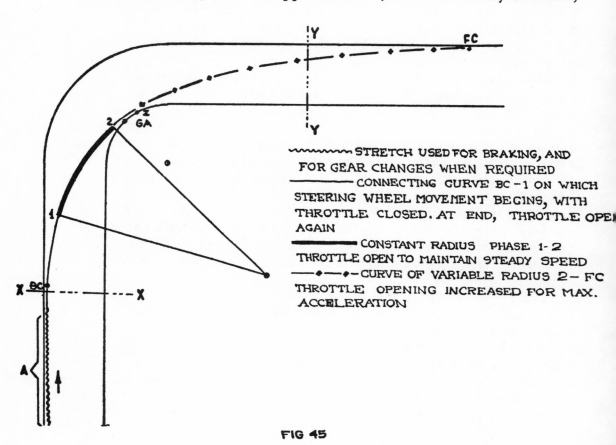

~~~~~~~STRETCH USED FOR BRAKING, AND FOR GEAR CHANGES WHEN REQUIRED
————————CONNECTING CURVE BC–1 ON WHICH STEERING WHEEL MOVEMENT BEGINS, WITH THROTTLE CLOSED. AT END, THROTTLE OPE AGAIN
━━━━━━CONSTANT RADIUS   PHASE 1-2 THROTTLE OPEN TO MAINTAIN STEADY SPEED
—•——•—CURVE OF VARIABLE RADIUS 2– FC THROTTLE OPENING INCREASED FOR MAX. ACCELERATION

FIG 45

inertia makes the car unwilling to rotate about its vertical axis and go into a drift. It is easier to initiate the turning moment, and cause the rear wheels to break away, if you go into the first part of the approach curve with the throttle shut, because the slight braking effect of the engine will take some of the weight off the back wheels and reduce their adhesion.

The initial movement of the steering-wheel must be very decisive and quick (one- or two-fifths of a second), both to take up any play in the

XXVII. Piero Taruffi in the winning car in the XXIVth Mille Miglia cornering fast on the Passo Futa.

XXVIII. *Top Left:* At Monza during the Italian G.P. of 1957: Hawthorn (Ferrari) and Bonnier (Maserati) on the South Curve. The large amount of lock required by the Ferrari for a relatively gentle corner shows how this motor car understeers. Compare the angle of Hawthorn's front wheels with that of Bonnier's. *Top Right:* Silverstone, 1958: Moss takes his Vanwall into Copse. Note the slightly understeering attitude that the car has taken up . . . *Bottom Left:* . . and the much more pronounced one adopted by Hawthorn's Ferrari . . . *Bottom Right:* . . . and by Peter Collins' Ferrari which won the race.

XXIX. Going into the South Curve at Monza: Fangio, Moss, Brooks, Lewis-Evans and Behra. Notice the different line taken by Fangio in number 2, master of the 'braking drift' approach.

XXX. *Above:* Monte Carlo, 1956: Stirling Moss at the wheel of a Maserati as he goes into Tobacconist's Corner. We are watching the first phase—the end of the approach curve; the wheels are being locked over to their fullest extent.

Below: ... and Stirling Moss again in a Vanwall, 1958.

mechanism, and to get the car 'laid over' for the corner; afterwards, when the front wheels have started to drift, turn it more gently and slowly.

Once the car has begun to turn and the rear end has broken away, it will tend to go on doing so through inertia, and during the second part of your approach curve you must check this tendency: you will begin to accelerate as required, partly to bring the weight back aft, and increase, inversely at first, the adhesion of the rear wheels. It is during the first phase that the angle of drift gets gradually larger, and the steering-wheel is turned through its greatest angle. Great care must be taken in choosing BC, the spot where you start to go in, because, after Z, it is the most important point on the whole corner. Bear in mind that the faster the corner, the longer must be the approach curve and the slower the movement of the steering-wheel.

THE MIDDLE PHASE   In the constant-radius phase it is best to keep the engine pulling, with just enough throttle to hold the car at a steady speed and in a controlled four-wheel drift. You should try to maintain equilibrium between the three forces acting upon it. On touring cars, and others of low power/weight ratio, one often needs full throttle during this phase, simply to keep the car going at a constant speed. In such cars the power of the engine, particularly on fast bends, is barely enough to overcome the resistances set up by drift, added to all the other kinds of drag met with in the ordinary way.

It may be interesting to note, from the accompanying graphs, the amount of drag set up by the tyres at various slip angles.

The first shows the amount of power required to take a car, each wheel of which carries a weight of 950 lb, through a corner at speeds of 40 to 80 m.p.h.

The second shows the engine power required by the car to take a corner at 37 m.p.h. with different loadings up to 2,000 lb per tyre.

It is in the middle phase of the corner that the driver should pay more attention so as to contact his 'clipping point' and settle the exact moment (in cars of high power) to start accelerating away.

Some variation in the amount of throttle-opening and some movements of the steering are inevitable, if only because the road surface is irregular and therefore offers a constantly changing grip. A driver has to make his corrections at lightning speed, and it is these movements which give him the 'feel' of the road and tell him what his front wheels are going to do as speed approaches the limit. These 'corrections' should not be overdone; too much sawing at the wheel is tiring—and besides, it looks untidy.

The theoretically correct amount of lock is that provided by the steering geometry, increased or reduced according to the under or oversteering

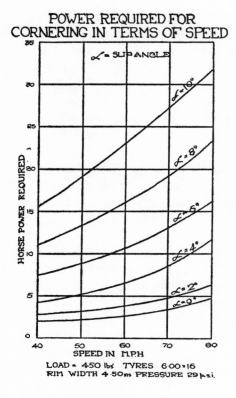

POWER REQUIRED FOR
CORNERING IN TERMS OF SPEED

FIG 46a

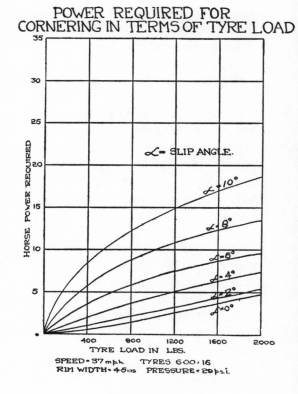

POWER REQUIRED FOR
CORNERING IN TERMS OF TYRE LOAD

FIG 46b.

characteristics of the car. On fast corners, where considerable engine torque is required merely to hold the speed constant, cars may often be observed in attitudes of oversteer.

THE LAST PART OF THE CORNER This part should be devoted wholly to acceleration. Here the power/weight ratio of the car is of great importance. Upon it depend the shape of the variable-radius exit curve and the amount of throttle required; the latter, as we have seen, is what supplies any forward thrust, and, in extreme conditions, it can also reduce the side thrust that the tyres receive from the road.

Very potent machines are therefore the most difficult to drive, and people coming to them direct from less powerful cars, in which they have been used to 'banging the throttle wide open', will find themselves heading straight for a dangerous *tête à queue* if they try the same game. Knowing when to open up is something which one only acquires by degrees. For this reason it may be wise, especially to start with, to stay in a higher gear; you avoid the troubles we have been discussing, and you save the time that would have been taken up by an extra gear-change as you come into the straight.

In gentle touring cars you have to put your foot hard down. In cars having a power/weight ratio of 80–100 b.h.p./ton on surfaces with a factor of ·6 to ·7, and in a gear giving 40–50 per cent of the car's maximum speed (second for example), you have to use the accelerator with discretion, and accentuate the expanding radius of your exit curve even more.

All European touring cars have a power/weight ratio a good deal lower than this. The M.G. Magnette, for example, has about 60 b.h.p. per ton. On almost all sports cars the figure varies between 100 and 250. On Formula I racing cars it reaches a maximum of 330–400 and on racing motor-cycles around 330. These figures are for vehicles in running condition.

On many sports cars, and most racing cars, special self-locking differentials are fitted, which do not allow the inside rear wheel to spin when weight is taken from it by centrifugal force as the car accelerates out of a corner. Handling cars with a self-locking diff. for the first time, you may find them somewhat tricky, but the difficulties are soon overcome. You get a feeling that the car is unwilling to answer the helm. The usefulness of this device, however, on machines of good power/weight ratio, is indisputable. It is a 'must' if your car is really potent.

I have lingered over these matters to give some rough idea of the problems involved. The really important thing is that, once you open up again halfway round the corner, you must not lift your foot for any reason at all—either through coming in too fast, taking the wrong line, accelerating too hard, or miscalculating the slipperiness of the road surface on the way out. You can sometimes hear people making this mistake if you listen as cars come out of a corner; drivers who 'blip' are not getting the most from their cars.

During this stage some steering lock is taken off, either because you wish to run wider, or because engine torque is making the car oversteer. Thus, while the back of the car is still on the 'limit', the front is not, and therefore it is necessary to give a smaller slip angle to the front wheels. You can watch this happening as cars accelerate out of a corner: the driver, if already on the limit, is compelled to take off some lock.

In cornering, the wheel should never be turned more than is strictly necessary. If you turn it too far in one direction in correcting a mistake, it simply means you have to turn it back again. The final result is an unnecessary waste of human energy and a more or less serious drop in maximum speed through the corner. Do not be unduly impressed, therefore, by drivers who saw away at the wheel, either because they think it makes them go faster or because they want to show off.

UNDERSTEERING CARS   In cars with this characteristic, the steering wheel has to be turned further during the entry phase for a given corner taken at high speed. This unwillingness to answer the helm is specially marked in heavy cars at high moments of inertia and at large angles of roll.

In the second phase of the approach curve, and throughout the constant-radius stage, the car is held to a steady speed with the throttle, and has no tendency to break away at the back. If the understeering characteristics are very marked, it will, in fact, tend to break away at the front, especially on surfaces giving a poor co-efficient of adhesion.

On curves of short radius, when the front wheels are locked right over, inertia makes the vehicle understeer more than ever, and this can easily bring about a front-wheel skid during the entry phase, so that the car goes on at a tangent. As we have seen, the driver can use his throttle to vary the amount of sideways thrust that the tyres receive from the road; he can reduce the understeering characteristic and even convert it to oversteer by spinning the back wheels and so reducing their adhesion. This trick can be used with effect on hairpin bends, where the understeer is most marked. If you judge it properly, there will be a slight rear-end breakaway and the corner can be taken faster.

OVERSTEER   During the first part of the entry phase you turn the wheel faster, but through a smaller arc. The car has a greater tendency to corner. Cars with a high moment of inertia are made easier to corner by oversteer.

Quite early in stage two of the approach curve, when you have to open up, you must start turning the wheel the other way. This need for 'unwinding' makes itself felt even more during the last phase of the corner, when the car is accelerating away on full throttle. For the reason mentioned above, this property facilitates handling on sharp corners.

The type of suspension and its springing characteristics, the height of the centre of gravity, the polar moment of inertia, wheelbase, track and many other design details exert an influence on roadholding, making the car easy or less easy to drive, and determining the degree of over or understeer.

Cars which have a 'neutral' tendency, or a slight degree of understeer, give the best results and therefore all modern cars are designed with these characteristics.

BEYOND THE LIMIT   When cornering rapidly it can happen, through excessive speed or an unexpectedly slippery patch of road, that the two front wheels, or the two back wheels, or even all four, lose their grip. In that case the car gets into an uncontrolled slide.

Generally it is the back wheels that lose adhesion in this way, and the rear part of the car starts sliding towards the outside of the corner. Fortunately the sudden increase in slip angle that this entails will set up increased resistance and slow the car down, often giving you a chance to regain control. You must now 'unwind' the steering immediately, to bring the car back in the right direction. At the same time you should apply a little engine torque to induce a slight pitching movement, thus transferring weight to the rear wheels. To lift your foot right off, or, worse still, use the brakes (and also, on very powerful cars, to open the throttle too wide) will turn an already desperate situation into disaster. The effects of the rear-end breakaway are a loss of speed and a lengthening of the theoretically correct course. As it loses speed, the car becomes more controllable and you are then in a position to steer it round the corner in the normal way, having lost precious time in the meanwhile. If, however, you have gone a long way past the limit of adhesion, the car will spin off at a tangent, and you will have nothing to do but sit and hope.

When it is the front wheels that go, the car tends to slide straight on, at a tangent to the corner. In this situation you can only lift your foot and turn the steering so that the wheels are pointing straight, hoping that they will regain their grip before the car goes off the road; if this succeeds you must lock over again to get round the corner. This usually happens on very understeering cars when the road surface suddenly offers less grip, as for example when changing from a dry road on to a patch of wet.

A car that 'loses' its front wheels first creates one of the most unpleasant sensations to be found in racing, because once it goes 'over the limit' it is very hard to bring back.

KNOWING ONE'S CAR   Every type of car is differently constructed, with different design features and therefore different handling characteristics. You just have to get to know your mount and adapt yourself to it.

This is especially important when driving strange cars. The first things to find out are the time it takes to 'lay over' and how much it tends to 'break away' at the front or at the back. The former will help to tell you the correct

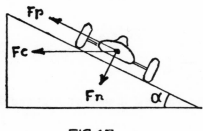

FIG 47

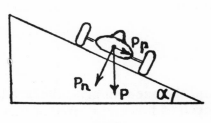

FIG 48

93

length for the approach curve, the latter whether to begin this manœuvre early or late.

The best way of finding out this 'laying over' or 'roll factor' is to take a series of S-bends; the tendency to break away with the front or back wheels can be ascertained, fairly safely, on corners of short radius, like hairpin bends. To get the feel of these limitations as quickly as possible, I advise making the test on an aerodrome; if you cannot do this, choose a winding stretch of road with sharp corners. S-bends can also be practised on a straight piece of road, if it is at least 25 feet wide. Obviously during these evolutions one should have the road all to one's self!

I hope these suggestions, plus a lot of practical work on a circuit or aerodrome, will be of assistance to learners in developing their own natural gifts and in getting to know their cars in the least possible time.

3 · Banked Corners

A factor which increases the speed at which a corner can be taken is 'superelevation', or banking of the road. The amount of banking to be found on ordinary roads seldom exceeds a few degrees from the horizontal, but on racing tracks it can be very steep; at Montlhery and Monza, for example, the maximum angle θ of banking is 40° and 38° respectively.

This inclination greatly increases the speed for the corner because the centrifugal force Fc, which acts horizontally on the car, is composed of two separate entities, a component Fp, acting parallel to the sloping face of the banking and less than Fc, and a second force Fn at right angles to the road surface, which further increases the weight pressing the car down upon the road (see fig. 47).

Moreover, the weight of the car P, which acts in a vertical direction, also comprises two factors, a force Pn at right angles to the track acting in conjunction with Fn, and a force Pp parallel with the track surface which serves to reduce Fp, the component of centrifugal force also acting parallel with the banking (fig. 48).

You may care to know the formula that gives the maximum speed for a corner, expressed in terms of the co-efficient of adhesion f, the radius of the curve r and the angle of banking θ:

$$V = \sqrt{\frac{\sin \theta + f \cos \theta}{\cos \theta - f \sin \theta}\ g\ r}$$

and the one that gives the weight of the car for various speeds on a curve of given radius and degree of banking:

$$Pn = P \cos \theta + Fc \sin \theta$$

94

To make things clearer I have prepared graphs from these formulae (figs. 49 and 50), assuming adhesion factors of ·5 and ·7.

In practice, it is not these considerations that limit speed on the bankings, but the bumps. These tracks give you a very rough ride if you are not in good training and if you have to drive cars with insufficiently developed suspension systems. On very high speed corners the suspension is subject to loadings almost double those met with on the straight (fig. 50), and must therefore be designed with a variable rate.

Especial care must be taken to avoid the worst of the bumps. By going higher or lower on the banking, when speed permits, you should manage to pick the best course. It is a good plan, all the same, to go into training so that you can physically cope with the effect of bumps that alternately press you down in the seat and leave you hanging in the air. The driving position and the driving seat should be designed with the greatest care. A shoulder harness is extremely useful, I find.

Apart from this bumping, banked corners present no great difficulty; the main thing is that drivers need a certain amount of practice before they get over the feeling that they are being squashed against the banking by centrifugal force.

In this sort of driving one does not try to 'cut' the corners, and take a special 'line' as one does on the flat. At tracks like Monza and Montlhery, the curves turn through an arc of 180° and the banking steepens sharply towards the outside. The conventional way of taking them is to go round with the outside wheels at a constant distance from the edge, as at A in fig. 51.

The distance from the outside edge depends on the speed of the car. Parallel lines are painted on the track to assist in maintaining direction, and therefore the correct height.

For any given height on the banking there is a corresponding speed at which the car will go round 'hands off'; this is the speed at which the resultant R of the weight P and centrifugal force Fc is at right angles to the track (fig. 52).

At this speed the car, even if left to itself, tends to steer a course that passes through those points; this is the 'ideal' line where losses are at a minimum, and therefore the one to choose for any given speed, as we can see from the graph (fig. 53). If you wish to go higher or lower on the banking without altering speed, you must do so by turning the steering-wheel.

When driving at speeds above this 'ideal' maximum (V = 114 m.p.h. in the example shown in fig. 53), it is not a good plan, in my opinion, to come down the banking to where the slope is less steep. True, there is a smaller percentage increase in the total weight of the car (see graph fig. 50) but one must bear in mind that the outside tyres and suspension elements are being

95

subject to much higher loadings than the inside ones. One should really only do this in cars of Indianapolis type, in which the weight has been purposely concentrated on the side nearest the inner edge of the track, and the springing on the 'outside' has been specially reinforced.

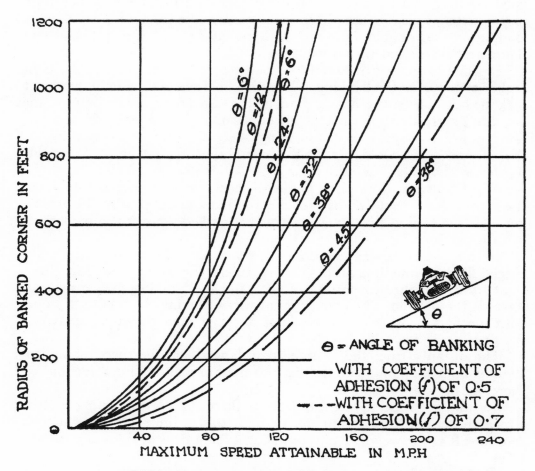

SPEED ON BANKED CORNERS
FIG 49

On first acquaintance with this sort of track, it is a good plan to start by lapping low down, at the 'natural' speed for your height, and gradually climb the banking as your speed builds up. If you drive round the top of the banking slowly, and therefore without the assistance of centrifugal force, the car will tend to slide down towards the inner edge.

96

XXXI. Fangio in the final phase, opening up as he leaves a right-hand corner. The front wheels are locked over to the left: oversteer due to the rapid acceleration.

XXII. Stirling Moss (30) and Masten Gregory, both on Coopers, photographed coming out of the Gasworks Hairpin Monaco in 1959.

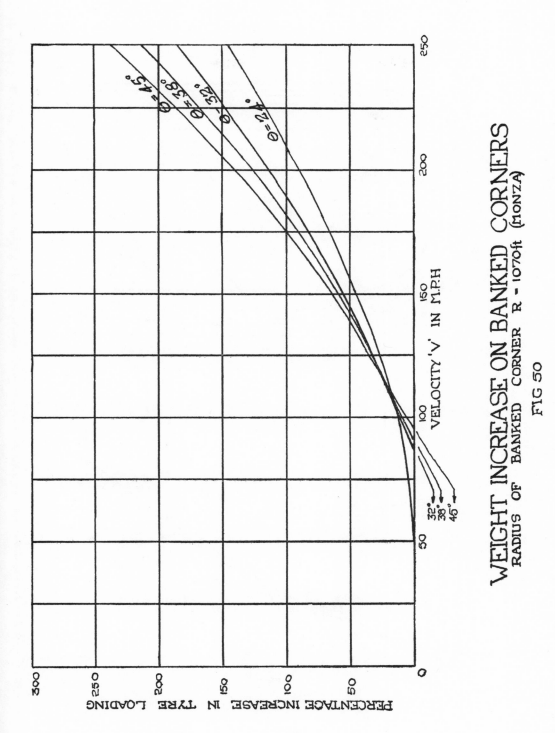

WEIGHT INCREASE ON BANKED CORNERS
RADIUS OF BANKED CORNER R - 1070ft (MONZA)
FIG 50

97

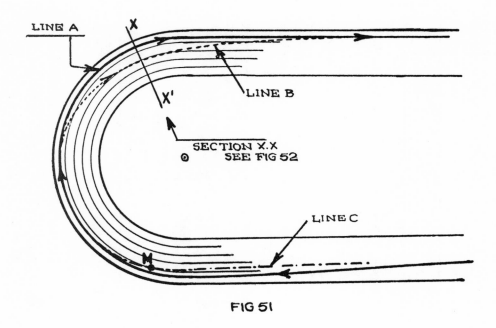

LINE A

X

LINE B

X'

SECTION X.X
SEE FIG 52

LINE C

M

FIG 51

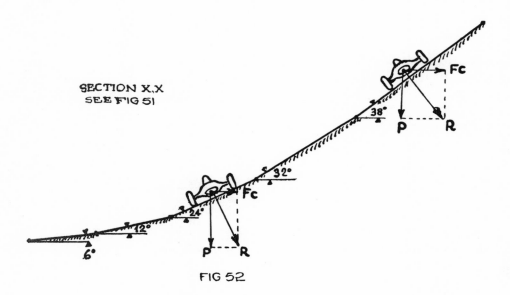

SECTION X.X
SEE FIG 51

Fc

38°

P

R

Fc

32°

24°

12°

6°

P

R

FIG 52

When lapping very fast, however, and therefore at speeds beyond the 'natural' maximum for the corner, one has to plan one's approach, and, even more important, one's exit line from the corner, with the greatest possible care. If you do not take active steps to leave the corner on the right 'line', you may find, as you come off the banking and therefore lose the support of centrifugal force, that the car will lose adhesion as it drives on to the straight.

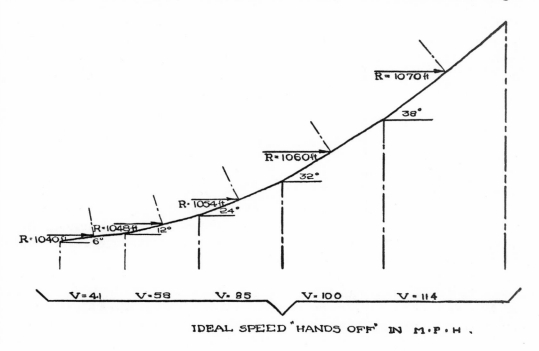

IDEAL SPEED "HANDS OFF" IN M·P·H·

FIG 53

If you find this happening, start coming off the banking before the end of the curve, in the way shown (considerably exaggerated) in fig. 51.

In very fast cars the part that has always impressed me most is coming into the corners, and the safest line, I find, is the one shown dotted as C in fig. 51. You get a fairly sharp jolt at the point M, but you do avoid being left in the air owing to slight variations in slope at the point where the banking merges into the straight, as happens if you follow the course marked A. I think this line also pays from the lap-time point of view—and it certainly *feels* the safest.

Because of the high speeds, and therefore the extra high loadings that a banked track makes possible, one must pay great attention to the state of one's tyres, and make sure that, if oversize covers have not been fitted, the existing ones have been inflated above the normal pressure.

99

In the wet, banked curves are far safer than the flat ones, chiefly because when the banking is very steep, the centrifugal component acting parallel to the plane of the banking is considerably smaller than the force of adhesion. Also, because rainwater running off the steep parts of the banking washes away the film of dust and slime that nearly always accumulates at corners on the flat.

Owing to the friction that is generated by the car's increased weight while in the corner, there is a speed loss which may be as much as 5 per cent or more. To recapture this speed as soon as possible I have found it a good plan to come out of the corner on line A, since you can exploit the dive off the banking. This is also a good line when you want to overtake a competitor; it succeeds best when the latter has chosen to come out on line B.

4 · *Donkey's Back Roads*

Some roads are built with a steep camber, so that rainwater will drain away easily; this, too, will call for some alteration in cornering technique.

Taking the classic line of maximum radius, as described earlier for flat roads, a car on a cambered road will go into the corner on an unfavourable slope, enjoy the benefit of mild 'banking' during the middle section and come out once more on a road that is 'banked the wrong way'.

As we saw in the section on banked corners, any transverse slope of the road will, for a given radius, affect the maximum speed at which the corner can be taken. Being unable (or unwilling in this case) to alter his speed, a driver has no alternative but to adapt himself to the corner by altering its radius: increasing it on the stretch BC–1 and 2–FC, where the slope is against him, and reducing it between 1 and 2, where the slope is in his favour.

To achieve this path, one has to lock over a little sooner (at B′C) than one would on a perfectly flat road (BC) and turn the steering-wheel more slowly. In other words, a longer approach. The steeper the camber, and the more slippery the road, the more you have to allow.

On wet roads, and worse still on ice, the car's course has to be considerably modified. Let us take an illustration: If the co-efficient of adhesion is ·1, for example (and as we have seen, it can be even lower than this on black ice), and the negative banking is more than 10 per cent, the car will tend to slide sideways even on the straight. In such cases you cannot expect to take any sort of 'corner', even on the longest radius. Should you find yourself in this position you must drive on the crown of the road where the slope is nil, and start your corner from the centre instead of from the outside. In this case you will get no help except from the favourable camber on the

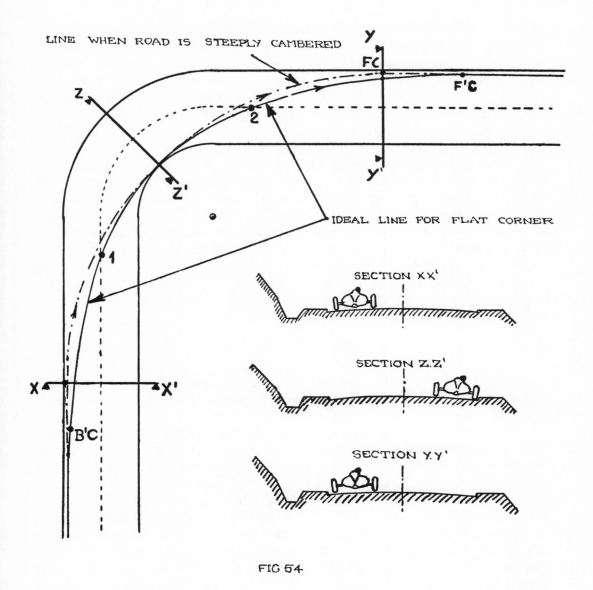

LINE WHEN ROAD IS STEEPLY CAMBERED

IDEAL LINE FOR FLAT CORNER

SECTION X X'

SECTION Z.Z'

SECTION Y.Y'

FIG 54

inside of the corner. This is a special case that one only comes across on roads of extreme slipperiness.

On certain roads, where the adhesion factor is as low as ·4 or ·3, one comes pretty close to the above situation. In these conditions you have to vary your radius a lot, taking a wide sweep where the slope is against you, and going slightly less wide where the slope is favourable. At the most, a camber slope of 5 per cent will have the same effect as a change of ·05 in the

101

adhesion factor, an amount which must be added to or subtracted from the actual factor for the road at the time, according to which way the camber slopes. This difference is most easily felt when the road surface is slippery, as, for example, in the wet.

Let us take two examples: imagine a corner with the above degree of camber, and a surface such as wet asphalt, having a co-efficient of ·35. During the approach and exit phases, we must drive as we should on a corner that was uncambered, but possessed of a co-efficient of ·30 (i.e. ·35 − ·05). During the middle phase, on the other hand, we can reckon on an adhesion factor of ·40 (i.e. ·35 + ·05). This will mean a variation in the radius, as between the outer and central phases of our 'corner', amounting to about 33 per cent.

Now let us go through the same bend, but with an adhesion factor of ·7, as on dry tarmac. The two outer phases must be treated as though the road had a factor of ·65 (i.e. ·7 − ·05), but in the central part we can carry on as though the factor was ·75 (i.e. ·7 + ·05). In this case the total difference between the inner and outer phases will be only 15 per cent.

5 · *Roads of Varying Slopes*

'VERTICAL CURVES' On the road one sometimes meets with humps and hollows at places where uphill and downhill stretches join, or where either of these gives way to the flat.

The ideal line here, and consequently the limiting maximum speed, will differ from that used on the flat. When a change of slope is encountered, the car takes a 'corner' in the vertical plane, and centrifugal force is generated which will increase or diminish its grip on the road, depending on whether the slope becomes more steep or less so. In practice, when a racing driver comes upon a place where the road rises suddenly and steeply from the flat, he feels as if his body is being squashed into the seat and his car pressed down into the road. This pressure brings about an increased adhesion which, if you can turn it to account, will allow a higher speed through the corner than would be possible on a flat road. We are here on the threshold of 'space travel', which stands in the same relationship to ordinary driving as the university stands to the secondary school, or the Nürburgring to an aerodrome circuit.

The various tricks of the trade for dealing with this sort of circuit are something that cannot be taught. Obviously it is more difficult to find the 'limit' on an up-and-down sort of corner; courses which contain many of these take longer to learn and they also undeniably demand a higher standard of driving.

Let us take an example: supposing that halfway round the corner shown in fig. 55 the rise in the road gives a gradient variation of 10 per cent.

If the road were straight, the ideal course through this corner would follow the dotted line in the diagram—our old friend MCR, the 'curve of maximum constant radius', in this case a radius of 345 feet. Owing to the change in slope, however, we shall have to take a wider sweep than this on the first part of the corner, where it is flat, using a radius of roughly 425 feet. This will obviously allow us to go faster. In the second half of the

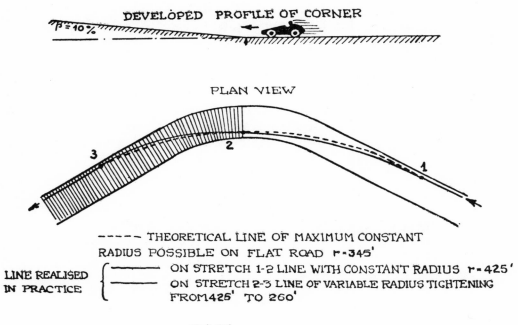

DEVELOPED PROFILE OF CORNER

PLAN VIEW

- - - - - THEORETICAL LINE OF MAXIMUM CONSTANT
RADIUS POSSIBLE ON FLAT ROAD r=345'

LINE REALISED
IN PRACTICE
⎰ ———— ON STRETCH 1-2 LINE WITH CONSTANT RADIUS r=425'
⎱ ———— ON STRETCH 2-3 LINE OF VARIABLE RADIUS TIGHTENING
FROM 425' TO 260'

FIG 55

corner, we can shorten the radius of our turn from 425 feet to 260, because the extra adhesion due to the gradient will permit the same speed as would a radius of 425 feet on the flat. This increase in adhesion is not instantaneous, because the springs transmit it to the ground progressively; this time-lag is naturally very brief, and it depends on the softness of the suspension, the shock-absorber setting, the ratio of sprung to unsprung weight, and so on. You have to be ready, therefore, to widen the radius again, quickly but gradually, the moment you feel the extra g come off the tail and the car beginning to slide. In complicated cases like this, you need long experience and extremely good 'hands'.

Another situation arises when a corner comes at the top of a hill (fig. 56).

If the vertical curve is very sharp and the car is going fast, it will 'take off' as it reaches the summit. In this case the first part (1–2) of the corner must be completed before the change of slope, so that the car is subject neither to inertia nor to centrifugal force as it leaves the ground. Otherwise it will tend to swing about its vertical axis during the whole of the stretch from 2 to 3, while it is off the ground. The trickiest time of all is the landing: the machine *must* come down straight! The stretch from 3 to 4 is completed after touching down, and it is very hard to take this bit 'on the limit'; the co-efficient of adhesion is very variable, as it depends on the way the car touches the ground, and how the springs absorb the shock. It is wise, therefore, to be a bit careful and keep within fairly safe limits, taking this second 'corner' on a wider radius.

UPHILL AND DOWNHILL CORNERS Even when the gradient is constant, hills will affect the speed at which a given corner can be taken, depending upon which way they slope. In this case, too, it is difficult to plan in advance because there are so many variable factors. When the tail begins to slide, one can say that an uphill slope is a help and a downhill one a

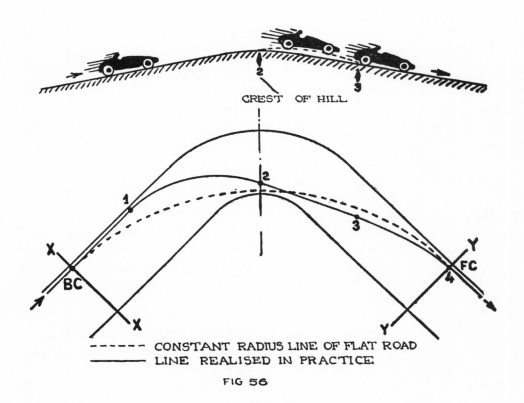

CREST OF HILL

- - - - - CONSTANT RADIUS LINE OF FLAT ROAD
———— LINE REALISED IN PRACTICE

FIG 56

XXXIII. *Above:* Collins at Copse. The rear wheels of the Ferrari have broken away, and the driver has had to apply opposite lock for correction. Inevitably the car has departed from the ideal 'line'.

Below: Same place, same marque and driver—but different mistake. This time the breakaway is at the front end; the driver will have to take off some lock immediately and lift his foot.

XXXIV. Two American machines on the banking at Monza during the 1957 500 miles.

Below: Italian G.P., 1955: Taruffi (14) and Kling, on the south banking at Monza, both driving Mercedes-Benz.

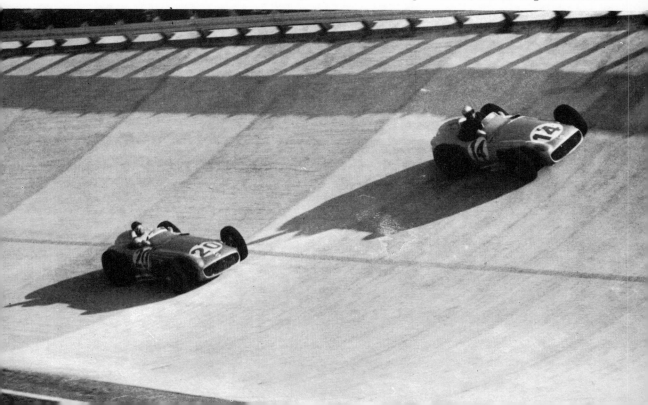

XXXV. *Above:* Piero Taruffi with his wife, Isabella, during a record session at Montlhéry in 1954. This was the first occasion that a Class I vehicle covered 200 kilometres in an hour. The car is the twin-boom TARF, and the engine is one of the famous 4-cylinder 500-c.c. Gileras, unsupercharged. In the background will be seen part of the banking.

Below: The twin-boom 500-c.c. TARF on the banking at Monza.

XXXVI. *Top Left:* Supercortemaggiore G.P. at Monza, 1956. Maestro Ugolini, racing manager of Maseratis, and Signora Taruffi hard at work with stop-watch and lap-chart. *Top Right:* . . . Knowing where you stand . . . Guerrino Bertocchi, of Maseratis, tells Jean Behra that he is leading in the British G.P. at Aintree in 1957; with Moss 40 seconds behind and 27 laps to go. When Behra retired the race went to Moss's Vanwall. *Bottom Left:* Belgian G.P., 1955: Meazza, of Ferrari's, gives Farina his position: third, with 13 seconds lead over Kling. *Bottom Right:* During the Italian G.P., 1955, a Mercedes mechanic signals to Fangio and Taruffi, who are almost side by side, that they stand first and second respectively, 41 seconds ahead of Castellotti's Ferrari, while Director Neubauer gives the order to drive 'regularly'.

hindrance; going downhill one has to be careful during the second half of the corner, especially if the road is not banked the right way.

Special attention is needed on downhill corners where the hill becomes steeper when you are halfway round. This is one of the occasions when it is easy to make the mistake of leaving the road at a tangent—tail first!

7

GENERAL ADVICE, PREPARATION AND TACTICS

LET ME START off by saying that the best way of breaking into racing is to begin right at the beginning—with something quite gentle and slow, like a 600 Fiat or perhaps an Austin Healey Sprite in standard tune. Then, if you have got what it takes, you can go on to faster cars. How long you will remain in the novice stage will depend on you; but if you are a real beginner, kick off with the car in which you feel most at home, even if this happens to be the family barouche: that's what I did!

If you have already competed a few times and want to take up racing seriously, look down the Calendar and consider very carefully which class and category are best suited to your ability. Take a lot of trouble over this; it may make all the difference between a decent racing career and your giving the whole thing up in disgust.

My advice is to start with a hill-climb. The course is short, so you can learn it really thoroughly, and discover exactly what you can and can't do with a minimum of unknown factors. There are no other competitors to put you off on the starting line or get in the way later on, so that you can concentrate more. Make the most of practice; and don't try and do too much. There is no point in leaving the road.

The preparation of your car is extremely important. Usually this has to be entrusted to tuning experts and mechanics, and everything will depend on them. They have a hard, tiring time of it, very often, working against the clock. But if they are real racing enthusiasts, like you, they will do a splendid job. All the same it is a good plan to let them share in any kudos and rewards that come your way. As they know every last detail about the car, they can give you useful tips about its weak points; after that it is up to you to get the best out of it, nursing it accordingly. If you work alongside the mechanics during the tuning period, you will pick up knowledge that will be enormously useful in getting the last ounce of performance during the race.

If you are just beginning, the pre-race atmosphere will be a great help. The mechanics, engineers and drivers whom you meet will always have something to teach you, and simply being with them will get you into the right mood. Try and make friends with one of them, and, if possible, follow him around in practice and during his races.

Read the regulations carefully before entering for an event, because it will be taken for granted that you understand them, and knowing them may save you from getting into trouble with the stewards, or being disqualified. Officials are there to look after the drivers' interests; avoid raising protests against their findings, which are made simply to ensure the success and smooth running of the meeting.

Make sure you know the meaning of the flag signals and that you can recognize them at any speed and even in the heat of conflict. Your life may depend upon it. The various flag signals are laid down in the International Sporting Code of the F.I.A., and they are as follows:

> *National flag:* Starting signal.
> *Blue flag held stationary:* Another competitor close behind.
> *Blue flag waved:* Another competitor wishes to overtake.
> *Yellow flag held stationary:* Danger. Slow down.
> *Yellow flag waved:* Serious danger, prepare to stop.
> *Red flag:* Stop immediately; race has been stopped.
> *White flag:* Service vehicle on circuit.
> *Yellow and red striped flag:* Oil on track.
> *Black flag with competitor's number:* Competitor to report at pits.
> *Chequered flag:* End of race, and all competitors to stop after crossing the finishing line.

Drive quietly and unobtrusively in the Paddock and when going to and from the scrutineers: you are not in the race yet. Above all, don't fancy yourself as a Speed King.

Do not forget your competition licence; it will be asked for.

In a long race see that you have the tools on board for make-shift repairs. In circuit racing this means practically no tools at all, except at Le Mans and events of that sort, where all repairs have to be carried out with tools carried on the car. In road races like the Mille Miglia carry at least a pair of pliers, a screw-driver, an adjustable spanner, some insulating-tape, some wire, and a few elastic bands, even if these are only bits cut from an old inner tube.

Wheel-changing equipment must be stowed where it is easy to get at; and take a 'chock' with you to stop the car running away if a wheel has to be changed on a hill. Practice wheel-changing until you can do it in the shortest possible time, and make sure that the jack will work properly even when the tyre is flat.

Take along some rubber tubing and a syphon device; they do not weigh much, and may be useful if you run out of fuel.

Consult the tyre people about what pressure they advise for the given conditions and see how the car handles with these settings before the race. Fast circuits and fast cars demand high pressures: otherwise you may throw a tread. This is not often dangerous but, if it should happen, watch out, because it will mean that even when you have put the spare wheel on you cannot risk using maximum speed on the straights until you have had an opportunity of replacing the spare. Tread-throwing sometimes originates through the tread separating at one point from the carcase of the tyre. There is nothing to be seen, but this sets up a noisy vibration which, when it happens in a rear tyre, can often be mistaken for trouble in the transmission.

Avoid starting a race with brand new tyres—they are slippery. They do not hold the road so well, and have caused a lot of accidents. If you have practised on tyres with say 40 per cent wear, you will have a dangerously exaggerated idea of the car's cornering power. It is therefore advisable to 'run in' new tyres before the start; and if the race is not one that depends upon tyre consumption, you will obtain the best results from covers that are more than 50 per cent worn. Use tyres with 'cut' treads only in the wet and on loose surfaces. On roads which afford a good grip, they are slightly slower on corners. I have discovered this by experience. It is extremely important to choose a type of tyre that suits the course on which it will be used; your speed through the swerves depends upon the 'cornering power' of your tyres, as explained in the previous chapter. Tyres also affect your speed on the straight, where smooth or ribbed treads are the free-est running. Tread patterns can easily make a difference of 2 to 3 per cent.

LEARNING A CIRCUIT   We have seen how the highest speeds are obtained by taking a properly planned 'line' through the corners; a matter that is not always easy on fast bends, some of which are 'blind'. One must first of all distinguish between little circuits that are only a few miles round, and long-distance road events. In the first case, you can begin your detailed study by obtaining a large-scale survey of the circuit. From this you can work out the radius of all the corners and the length of the straights; it will also give you the width of the road. If the course is hilly, calculating the best 'line' in every case may be a little tricky, but on flat roads it is simple enough. A first inspection, bearing in mind the accelerating powers of your motor car, may indicate the type of line to take through the various corners, since you know the length of the straights and the theoretical speed of each corner. These calculations will show you how much your 'clipping point' Z has to be moved in relation to the geometrical apex GA, which is easily identified on the plan; and if you are a bit dubious about your brakes, you can settle the places on the circuits where you can give them an easy time. Even if you do not feel inclined to go quite so minutely into things as this, I do advise you to make sure, by actual inspection of the circuit, that you have in mind the exact 'clipping point' Z for each of the corners. Once you have established this by practice, the rest will come instinctively. This knowledge can be acquired either by driving round the circuit a number of times, even in a touring car, or by inspecting each corner on foot and finding the exact spot by the methods outlined in Chapter 6. Even one such reconnaissance is an advanced lesson in itself. Standing on the ground you see all sorts of things that you would miss from a moving car: uneven patches, cambers that slope the wrong way, bits of slippery surface, and so on. In a car you can get a better idea of the circuit by driving round it at night, because the headlights make all the irregularities stand out. All these preparations should be over and done with before the roads are closed for the first official practising, so that you can embark on this with a thorough knowledge of the circuit.

When you start practising with the actual racing car, try and follow the correct 'lines' right away. One good way to find the 'limit' for a given bend, especially a fast one, is to bring the car to your cornering speed several hundred yards in advance. In this way you will not have to lift your foot, or, worse still, put the brakes on. Taking your speed from the speedometer or rev.-counter, go in a little faster each lap; this will make it easier to identify the 'clipping point' and reach it at exactly the right moment on a theoretically perfect line. Having learned the corner itself, now fix your braking points. Gear-changes will follow as a logical sequence: when the revs. reach the limit you have fixed, you change gear.

Some people work themselves into a state about which gear others use for a given corner. Why bother? It all depends on the gear ratios fitted and the speed at which the corner is taken. The main thing is to get maximum acceleration as you come *out* of the corner; but every gear-change that has to be made on the succeeding straight entails a loss of time, and this too has to be considered. It pays to take the corner in a higher gear much more often than you would think. This means one less gear-change to make during your approach, so that your braking is more decisive, and the same can be said for your approach line itself. On the whole I am rather against a lot of gear-changing; it is less hard on the transmission. I have noticed that changing down for every corner, even when it is unnecessary, and rushing along in low gear, is a weakness frequently found amongst beginners—and among those who want to show off!

To find the correct ratios, when it is possible to vary these, you should note the number of revs. that the engine will 'pull' on the longest straight on the circuit; the correct ratio will be that which allows the engine to reach maximum power in these conditions, or maximum safe revs. Remember, though, that in a race, when the engine and transmission have got really warmed up, the revs. will be 1 per cent or 2 per cent higher than they are after a few miles of practice. In plotting the ratios, bear in mind the length of the course and the amount of time that the engine will spend at full throttle. In a hill climb you can impose loads that would never do in a long race. You should also get the right ratio for the indirect gear that will be most often used.

When preparing for long-distance road races, devote all the time you have to recognizing features along the course. If you have not much time for this memory training, do not expect to do well, especially as it is risky to drive on the limit when you do not know the road. Lots of accidents have happened through skimpy preparation. Try therefore to get the most from what knowledge you have. On a completely strange circuit it will be a good idea to do a preliminary reconnaissance lap, to pick out the worst danger points and fix them in your mind, such as blind corners that 'tighten up' towards the end and gulleys that cannot be seen when you are driving fast.

The lie of the landscape may sometimes be quite a help: telegraph poles, for instance, often show which way the road goes—but do not count on this, because sometimes they march straight on across country, while the road jinks round a hidden corner! Whenever you come to a humpback bridge or switchback, memorize which way the road goes on the other side. You do not want to have to slow down unnecessarily and, equally, you do not want an accident.

If you have more time, study what I call the 'key' corners, i.e. those which lead into long pieces of straight.

If you mistake the 'line' through a corner that is followed immediately by another, the loss of time is insignificant—a few fifths of a second. A similar mistake at a 'key' corner may cost you a number of seconds, the time loss varying in direct proportion to the length of the ensuing straight and inversely with the amount of acceleration the car is capable of on coming out of the corner. You must make a point of learning these particular corners; study them during practice and concentrate on them in the race. When it comes to making a special effort or taking extra risks, do it here, where it pays best.

If the course is fairly long it is a good plan to learn it in stretches of a few miles at a time. Having committed one piece to memory, pass on to the next. The advantage of this system (and the length of the stretches) will of course depend on your memory. Concentrate on the stretches that have fast bends and the greatest number of 'key' corners. Familiarity with the last part of a long course may decide the race in your favour. There may be a rival who started ahead of you and now, for lack of pit signals, is 'taking it steady' or even slowing a bit, because he feels sure of his place. If you turn on the heat at the last you may take him by surprise. Fatigue during the last few miles causes much time to be lost, especially on roads which are not familiar; the moral of which is—learn the last bit thoroughly.

Here is the plan that I adopted when 'learning' a long-distance course: I found it is a good idea to drive over the course in short stretches of 3 to 6 miles, as described above. Turning round and retracing my steps, I used to pay attention only to the 'key' corners, which, taken in the reverse direction come *after* a piece of straight, and are therefore more easily identified. When going round the course in this way, you should get somebody else to drive the car so that you can give your entire attention to the 'key' corners, and photograph them on your memory. Next time over they will be taken in the right direction. When I had covered the route several times, following this routine, I used to find that I knew it fairly well.

Some drivers like to mark danger spots and special corners by painting marks on the road or, better still, on the retaining fence. Others employ a private code, with numbers and letters of the alphabet to convey a particular message: 'Caution', 'fast bend', 'don't lift your foot', 'this corner "tightens up" ', and so on, hoping that other drivers will not understand. It has been known, however, for such signs to disappear at the last minute, rubbed out by some unsportsmanlike adversary. This is one reason I have always mistrusted this system; the signs can easily be altered, in which case they are dangerous.

Others, with the help of a passenger, make notes of the entire course, corner by corner, with approximate speed for each, underlining any peculiarities. They turn these notes into a neat book, or transcribe the whole thing on to a roll of paper, which the passenger unrolls and reads out during the race. I have seen this system used by certain American drivers in the Carrera Panamericana, and in the Mille Miglia by Moss, Collins and Gendebien.

For myself, especially in recent years, I preferred not to take a passenger, and I was therefore compelled to carry the whole route, so far as possible, in my head. During practice I had a method of note-taking that allowed me to go over the course in my mind, aided by a good visual memory for corners.

RACE TACTICS Races are won not merely by going fast, but often by nursing one's strength and saving one's car better than the opposition. If your rival's car has a weak spot, try and make him overstrain it during the race; if he is at all an unstable type, take advantage of it. Some people get upset if another car sits close behind. Sooner or later they make a mistake and 'over-cook' either their car or a corner.

Very occasionally race tactics date back several days. Some people, though I do not approve of this, try to create an atmosphere of personal rivalry amongst competitors, hoping to turn this to account. Others, by a wisecrack, a sarcastic grin, or an ostentatiously confident air, try to upset a less thick-skinned rival, and make him start in a state of flap. Distrust such goings-on; they never do you any good! Then there are technical skirmishes between those responsible for preparing the cars, as they try to hide some 'mod.' of their own that they consider important, while trying to obtain data on other people's carburation, or gear-ratios, and pick up other hints that may save time during practice.

Right up to within a few seconds of the start, any sort of information about a dangerous rival can be of value: the possible mis-firing of his engine, the type of tyres fitted if the forecast says rain, and whether he will have to re-fuel.

Once the flag falls, you are all in it together, and it is up to everyone to behave in a thoroughly sporting manner, even towards—in fact especially towards—people they do not like. Back at the pits attempts are sometimes made to confuse members of a rival team by making ready for a pit-stop that will never take place.

In the assignment of pits, there is an advantage in having the end pit on the approach side; you get a good view of other people's signals, while your own pass pretty well unnoticed. Pit signalling must be done by experts, who are able to say, at any moment in the race, the number of seconds that separate you from the man in front or behind, how many laps remain till the end of the race, and where you stand in the general classification. The rest is less important. With this information to go on, you, who are the only person who knows the exact state of your car, can make up your mind what to do and what not to do.

Here is the system I found the best. On a circuit you want at least two people: one, armed with a split-hand stopwatch, to look after the lap-chart, the other to prepare the pit-signals and hold them out for the driver. Faster and Slower signals are much vaguer than this; but useful when something unexpected and important happens and there is no time to hang out a complete data board. A good pit staff can gain you a place and, what is more, it can save you from having to drive flat out when there is no need. Many races have been won or lost by the skill—or lack of it—of people in the pits.

In long distance road races, competitors are generally sent off at one minute intervals; to be among the last few, or anyway behind the most serious opposition, is highly convenient, because all the time one knows how the race is going. For early starters it is just the opposite, and this naturally affects the plan of campaign. The first man off becomes the fox. He will make splendid time if everything goes well for him; but if he wants to apply tactics he must lay on a highly efficient system of signalling, especially for the last part of the race. Here both telephone and radio are pressed into service.

Driving in hill-climbs, one has to give all one has got, but even here a signal station at half distance may be of value. Study every detail to get the maximum result. Put a chock behind a back wheel at the start, so that you do not need the handbrake on. On stretches where the surface is loose, be careful to avoid wheelspin; in powerful cars it pays to use the upper ratios much of the time. When the road affords a good grip, make very fast changes, taking the engine up past the revs. that give maximum power, always supposing the engine can stand it. Brake to the limit. It may pay to miss out the intermediate gears. Keep your foot down over the finishing line, but watch out, because sometimes there is not enough time or enough road in which to stop!

For my part, I like to time myself with a stopwatch on my wrist, setting it going exactly a minute before the Start. It is useful for telling me the time of the Start, and the times I set up during practice. If you are hoping to win and you have a rival whose times are close to your own, it may pay not to show your hand in practice; then he may not go flat out in the race, being lulled into a false sense of security.

On circuits where positions on the starting grid are governed by the times set up in Practice, one has got to put in at least one fast lap; but do not wreck the car in the attempt. The best lap times are done with the car running light: tank almost empty and tyres worn down to 50 per cent—and right at the last minute of Practice, so that your opponents cannot leap back in their cars and go one better!

How you actually drive in a race will depend upon the sort of car you have and your own capabilities and ambitions. It is better to drop one place in the results than to retire through over-driving, either because you have wrecked the engine or, worse still, run out of road. When possible try and take the lead; having the road to yourself is a great asset, one of the advantages being that you do not risk being involved in a pile-up caused by other competitors. If you can get in front, and immediately draw away from your rivals, this demonstration may dissuade them from pressing too hard. If you can build up a sufficient lead, the moment will come when you can slack off and take it easy. If, however, you cannot draw right away, let those behind set the pace. The best plan, I think, is to stay up among the leaders, so as to take advantage of any retirements, but all ready to attack during the last phase of the race. There is no point in going really hard in the opening stages, when statistics show that the majority of retirements take place in the first quarter of a race. These tactics will leave you with a machine in good condition for the final phase, when the field is reduced in size. This plan is not particularly glamorous, and will not bring you much glory if you yourself are among the people who pack up, but it is the most successful over a long run of races. What you are doing will not be appreciated by the general public, but neither will it be lost upon the people who really know, and upon those who supplied you with the car. It's up to you which group you would rather impress.

Whatever position you occupy in a race, the best plan is to just maintain any advantage you have, taking no more out of yourself and your machine than is strictly necessary. Force the pace or slow down according to what the man behind you does. Exert yourself only when there is a chance of gaining a place; here your pit signalling staff can be a great help.

There are unsporting types whose only idea is to win and who either retire, pretending their engine has blown up, when they see their hopes frustrated, or blow it up on purpose. A 'tell-tale' hand on the rev.-counter sometimes gives their game away.

As for young drivers, impatient to reach the top, I should like to remind them that a lot of people have had the worst accidents in their career through this kind of impatience. The most dangerous moment is after winning one's first race; one feels obliged to press on even harder and win again. This is the time to look out; and now I am talking not only to the drivers, but also to the friends they have about them: to the racing enthusiasts with whom they will be mixing, and their 'fans' who overpraise them and think them unbeatable. These people often do a lot of harm; they give drivers inflated ideas, and often urge them on to do things they should not attempt.

In racing a lot of people think they can keep up with the best, and say 'If I can once get level, I shall not let him get away'—and often the next thing is they go off the road! Driving behind someone with a machine of the same type can be a useful lesson in technique; but one has to remember that a man's speed depends not only on his personal skill, but also sometimes on the superior roadholding of his car—and against the latter there is nothing a driver can do.

Try to be a 'chronometer'. Every lap in exactly the same time. The skill of the great drivers consists to a great extent in this regularity.

If you should happen to slide off the road, or spin round in such a way that you are able to rejoin the race without outside assistance, do so with calm; undue haste can bring you into collision with other cars. If your car has had a 'shunt', have a quick look round it before starting off again: your own safety and other people's lives may depend upon it.

Pay attention, and do not let your mind wander. It may seem odd, but

114

many accidents are due to inattention. This can often happen in the course of a long race, as fatigue overtakes you without your even being aware of it. Step up your concentration, therefore, towards the end of the race.

Cautious tactics should be used more in very long distance races; I have often found them successful. The last occasion was in the Mille Miglia of 1957. With that great race I determined to close my career as an official works driver. If I succeed in maintaining this resolve I shall have done a wise thing—and one which I commend to my fellow veterans.

Finally, to the younger drivers for whom this book is written, I should like to say two things—not dry stuff like the contents of this manual, but speaking as one enthusiast to another.

In my view, the real sportsman is one who regards racing not as a means to an end, but as an end in itself. It is not the easy victory, it is worthwhile results that count—doing the best with the car at your disposal. It is not the title that makes the champion, but what he has got in him. I hope that my experience will be of use, and that this book may help some young enthusiasts to achieve their life's ambition.

BUENOS AIRES
LAP DISTANCE No.2 CIRCUIT 2.43 miles
LAP DISTANCE No.4 CIRCUIT 2.9 miles

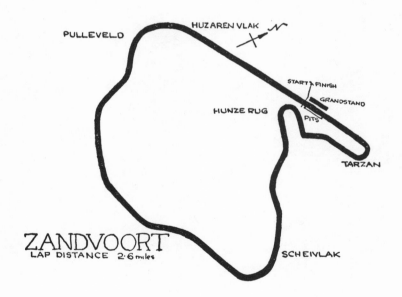

ZANDVOORT
LAP DISTANCE 2.6 miles

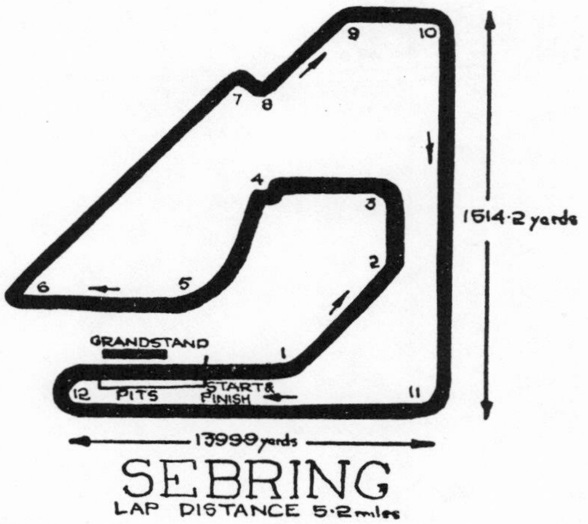
1
2
3
4
5
6
7
8
9
10
11
12
GRANDSTAND
PITS
START & FINISH
1514·2 yards
1399·9 yards
SEBRING
LAP DISTANCE 5·2 miles

WIPPERMANN
KARUSSELL
PLANZGARTEN
ADENAUER-FORST
FUCHSRÖHRE
SCHWALBENSCHWANZ
SCHWEDENKREUS
NURBURGRING
LAP DISTANCE 17·6 miles
N
QUIDDELBACHER HÖHE
ANTONIUSBUCHE
START & FINISH
SUDKEHRE

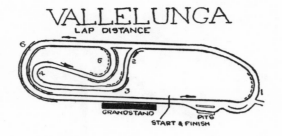

VALLELUNGA
LAP DISTANCE

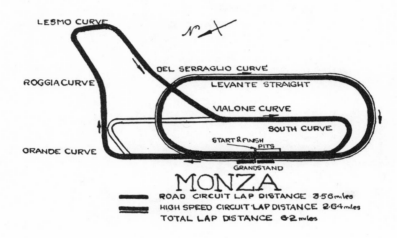

MONZA

ROAD CIRCUIT LAP DISTANCE 3·56 miles
HIGH SPEED CIRCUIT LAP DISTANCE 2·64 miles
TOTAL LAP DISTANCE 6·2 miles

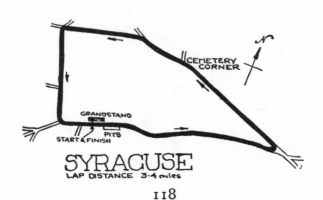

SYRACUSE
LAP DISTANCE 3·4 miles

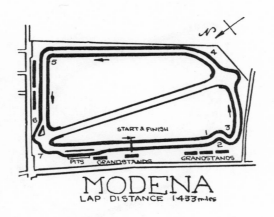

MODENA
LAP DISTANCE 1.433 miles

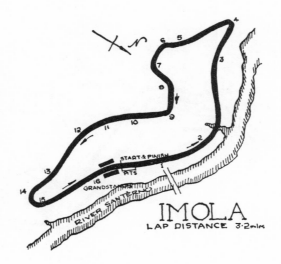

IMOLA
LAP DISTANCE 3.2 mls

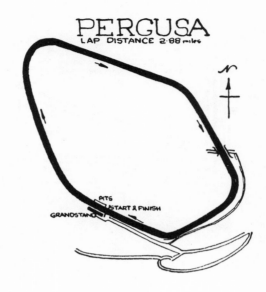

PERGUSA
LAP DISTANCE 2·88 miles

N

PITS
START & FINISH
GRANDSTAND

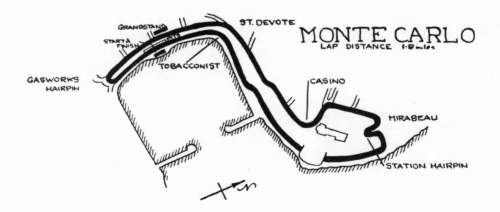

GRANDSTAND
ST. DEVOTE
MONTE CARLO
LAP DISTANCE 1·9 miles

START &
FINISH
PITS
TOBACCONIST
CASINO

GASWORKS
HAIRPIN
MIRABEAU

STATION HAIRPIN

N

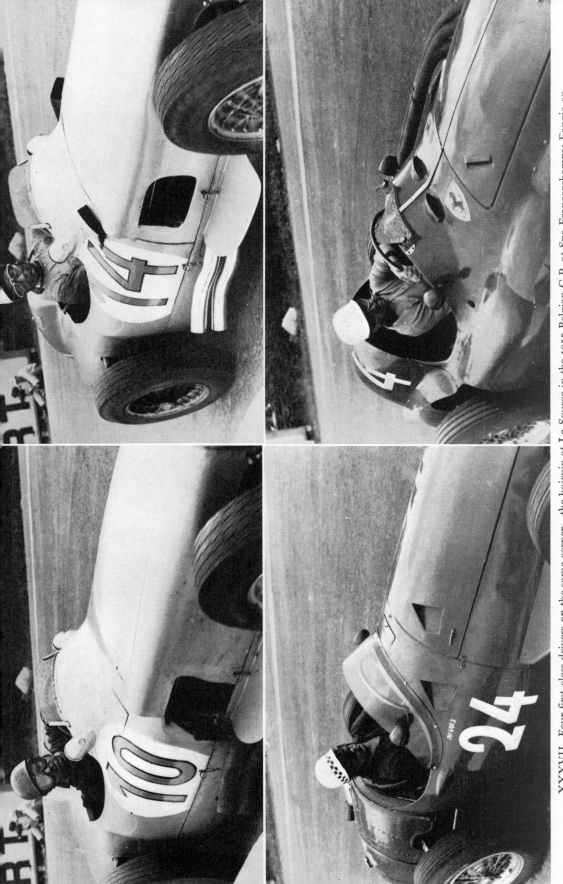

XXXVII. Four first-class drivers on the same corner—the hairpin at La Source in the 1955 Belgian G.P. at Spa-Francorchamps: Fangio on Mercedes number 10, Moss 14 Mercedes, Behra 24 Maserati, and Trintignant (Ferrari) number 4.

XXXVIII. At the G.P. at Morocco, Casablanca, 1958, four cars on the same spot: Number 8 is Moss's victorious Vanwall; the three Ferraris are driven by Mike Hawthorn (6), Phil Hill (4) and Olivier Gendebien (2).

XXXIX. Fangio (2) and Moss (6) in Mercedes-Benz, Ascari (26) and Castellotti (30) in Lancias going into Tobacconist's Corner at Monte Carlo, 1955.

XL. The flag with the black and white chequers is the one that means 'Race finished'. It is a flag that a driver always likes to see especially if he is first . . . as in this case! Piero Taruffi (number 535) and von Trips (number 532) cross the finishing line in the XXIVth Mille Miglia, 1957, first and second respectively.

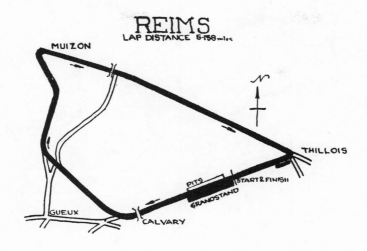

REIMS
LAP DISTANCE 5·158 miles

MUIZON

THILLOIS

PITS
START & FINISH
GRANDSTAND

GUEUX

CALVARY

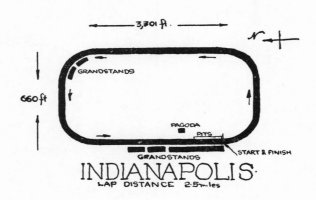

3,301 ft.

660 ft

GRANDSTANDS

PAGODA

PITS

GRANDSTANDS

START & FINISH

INDIANAPOLIS.
LAP DISTANCE 2·5 miles

LONG MADONIE
CIRCUIT OF SICILY
LAP DISTANCE 67.1 miles.

SHORT MADONIE
TARGA FLORIO
LAP DISTANCE 44.7 miles

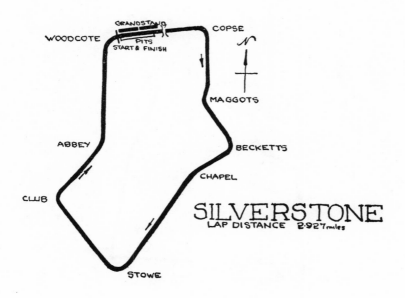

SILVERSTONE
LAP DISTANCE 2·927 miles

WOODCOTE
GRANDSTAND
PITS
START & FINISH
COPSE
N
MAGGOTS
ABBEY
BECKETTS
CHAPEL
CLUB
STOWE

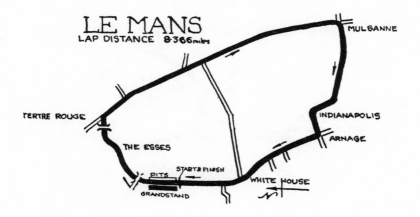

LE MANS
LAP DISTANCE 8·366 miles

MULSANNE
TERTRE ROUGE
INDIANAPOLIS
ARNAGE
THE ESSES
START & FINISH
PITS
GRANDSTAND
WHITE HOUSE

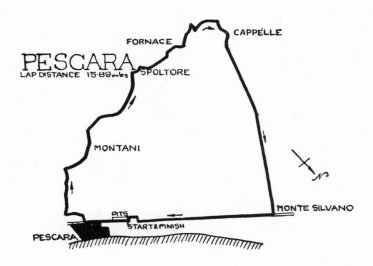

PESCARA
LAP DISTANCE 15·89 miles

FORNACE
CAPPELLE
SPOLTORE
MONTANI
MONTE SILVANO
PITS
START & FINISH
PESCARA

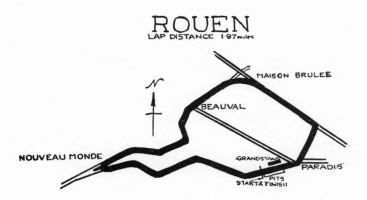

ROUEN
LAP DISTANCE 1·97 miles

MAISON BRULEE
BEAUVAL
NOUVEAU MONDE
GRANDSTAND
PARADIS
PITS
START & FINISH

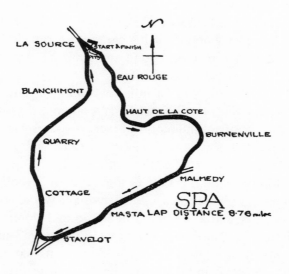

LA SOURCE
START & FINISH
EAU ROUGE
BLANCHIMONT
HAUT DE LA COTE
BURNENVILLE
QUARRY
COTTAGE
MALMEDY

SPA

MASTA LAP DISTANCE 8·76 miles

STAVELOT

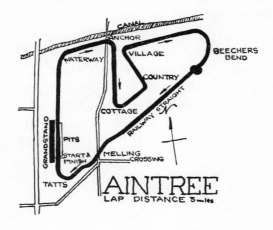

CANAL
ANCHOR
WATERWAY
VILLAGE
BEECHERS BEND
COUNTRY
COTTAGE
RAILWAY STRAIGHT
GRANDSTAND
PITS
START & FINISH
MELLING CROSSING
TATTS

AINTREE

LAP DISTANCE 3 miles

ABOUT THE AUTHOR

THERE CAN BE NO MAN in motor racing better qualified to write a book upon the art of motor racing than Piero Taruffi, born in Rome, Italy on October 10th 1906. The brief synopsis of his career (set out below) on both the sporting and the technical side proves beyond any doubt his fitness to speak upon both the theory and the practise of motor racing.

Like many great drivers before him, Taruffi drove both cars and motorcycles and won his first race on two wheels in 1925, when 19 years old. In forty-one races he scored twenty-two wins, twenty of them outright, and two only were class victories; amongst his principle successes were the 1928 Royal G.P. of Rome on Norton 500, a marque on which he also won the 1932 G.P. of the F.I.C.M. and the Montenero G.P. On C.N.A. Rondine he won the 1935 Grands Prix of Tripoli and Pescara.

In addition to his racing activities he broke thirty-eight Worlds records including those of the Flying Kilometre at 274 Km.h., the Standing Kilometre, the Standing Mile and the One Hour record also fell to him on Gilera in 1937 and 1939. On four wheels his record is even more impressive and in 136 races he scored forty-four wins of which fourteen were in class, and thirty in general classification. His first victory was in 1923 and his principle successes include the G.P. of Berne in 1948, the 1951 Carrera Panamericana Mexico, and in 1952 he won the Grand Prix of Switzerland and the Ulster Trophy. In 1954 he won the Targa Florio and the Tour of Sicily, which he also won the following year. In 1956 with Moss, Behra and Schell he shared the winning wheel in the 1000 Kilometre Race at Nurburg and in 1957 set the seal upon his brilliant career by winning the Mille Miglia.

In 1947 Taruffi was Champion of Italy (Racing Cars up to 1500 c.c.), and 1949 Formula 2 Champion of Italy. In 1951 he was the 5th in the Driver's World Championship, and 3rd in 1952. In 1954 and 1956 he was Italian Sports Car Champion. In addition to these honours he holds or has held thirty-nine International speed records and has been a member of the following official works teams: Scuderia Ferrari (1931, 1932, 1933), Maserati (1934, 1956, 1957), Bugatti (1955), Scuderia Ambrosiana (1937, 1938, 1939), Alfa Romeo (1939), Cisitalia (1947, 1948, 1949), Ferrari (1950, 1951, 1952, 1955, 1957), Lancia (1953, 1954), Mercedes (1955) and General Motors (1957).

In 1933 he obtained his Doctorate of Industrial Engineering in Rome and his technical appointments in the motor industry are no less formidable than his successes in the sporting side. He was racing manager and on the engineering staff of the C.N.A. Rondine concern from 1935-1937, and technical and racing manager for Gilera in 1937-1940. In 1946 and 1947 he was racing director, technical consultant and Chief Tester to Cisitalia and in 1950 rejoined Gilera as racing manager and technical consultant until 1956.

From this vast wealth of experience Piero Taruffi has crowned his career with the authorship of this book, *The Technique of Motor Racing*, which must rank as a standard work of reference to all who aspire to fame in the most fascinating, exciting and dangerous sports of all time.

NOTES

NOTES